NATURE'S DEADLIEST CREATURES

VISUAL ENCYCLOPEDIA

Penguin Random House

DK Delhi

Senior Editor Suefa Lee
Project Art Editor Pooja Pipil
Editor Isha Sharma
Assistant Art Editor Kanupriya Lal
Jacket Designer Tanya Mehrotra
Jackets Editorial Coordinator Priyanka Sharma
Senior DTP Designer Harish Aggarwal
DTP Designers Sachin Gupta, Rajdeep Singh
Picture Researcher Vishal Ghavri
Managing Jackets Editor Saloni Singh
Picture Research Manager Taiyaba Khatoon
Pre-production Manager Balwant Singh
Production Manager Pankaj Sharma
Senior Managing Editor Rohan Sinha
Managing Art Editor Govind Mittal

DK London

Editor Jessica Cawthra
Designer Chrissy Barnard
US Editor Kayla Dugger
Jacket Editor Claire Gell
Jacket Designer Surabhi Wadhwa-Gandhi
Jacket Design Development Manager Sophia MTT
Producer, Pre-production Siu Yin Chan
Senior Producer Angela Graef
Managing Editor Francesca Baines
Managing Art Editor Philip Letsu
Publisher Andrew Macintyre
Art Director Karen Self
Associate Publishing Director Liz Wheeler
Design Director Phil Ormerod
Publishing Director Jonathan Metcalf
Special & Custom Publishing Manager Michelle Baxter

Written by Derek Harvey
Consultant: Dr. Kim Bryan

This paperback edition, 2018
First American Edition, 2018
Published in the United States by DK Publishing
345 Hudson Street, New York, New York 10014

A catalog record for this book is available
from the Library of Congress.

ISBN 978-1-4654-8074-3

DK books are available at special
discounts when purchased in bulk for sales promotions, premiums,
fund-raising, or educational use. For details, contact: DK Publishing
Special Markets, 345 Hudson Street, New York, New York 10014
SpecialSales@dk.com

Printed and bound in China

A WORLD OF IDEAS:
SEE ALL THERE IS TO KNOW

www.dk.com

NATURE'S DEADLIEST CREATURES

VISUAL ENCYCLOPEDIA

CONTENTS

1

2

3

4

DANGER FACTOR

Our danger factor rates creatures from across a wide range of species and includes both those that are deadly in attack and those that are deadly in defense. The scale goes from a rating of 1 to 5.

Creatures that are given a rating of 1 are the least deadly.

Creatures that are given a rating of 5 are the most deadly.

5

DECEIVERS AND TRICKSTERS 98

6

DEADLY NUMBERS 124

7

SKILLS, TACTICS, AND CUNNING

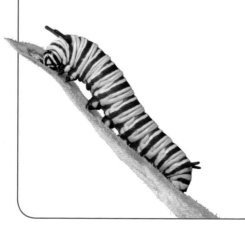

8

DISEASE AND DESTRUCTION

DEADLY CREATURES

Animals can be deadly for many different reasons—some in attack and some in defense. But they vary a lot in the risk they pose to other living things—including humans.

Deadly in all sizes

Any animal that can kill another organism can be classed as deadly. Some are only deadly to tiny insects or minute animals such as ocean plankton, while others are deadly on a much larger scale. Only a few are dangerous to humans.

Small killers, small victims
The smallest animals are usually deadly to other small animals. This spider's venom kills other spiders, but its bite cannot harm anything bigger.

Small killers, big victims
There are exceptions. This blue-ringed octopus is not much bigger than your fist, but its venom is strong enough to kill a human.

Big killers, big victims
Animals that combine massive size; physical strength; and large weapons, such as teeth, can sometimes be the deadliest of them all.

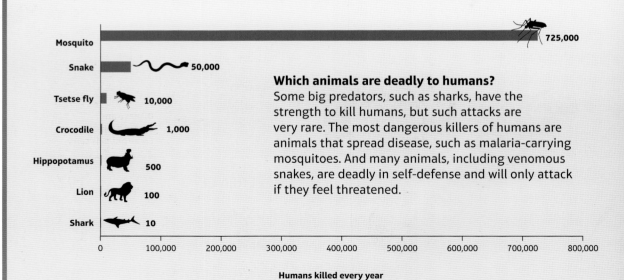

Animal	Humans killed every year
Mosquito	725,000
Snake	50,000
Tsetse fly	10,000
Crocodile	1,000
Hippopotamus	500
Lion	100
Shark	10

Humans killed every year

Which animals are deadly to humans?

Some big predators, such as sharks, have the strength to kill humans, but such attacks are very rare. The most dangerous killers of humans are animals that spread disease, such as malaria-carrying mosquitoes. And many animals, including venomous snakes, are deadly in self-defense and will only attack if they feel threatened.

What makes animals deadly?

Very different behaviors have evolved to make animals deadly, including methods of getting food and ways of escaping danger. Those that get their nutrition by killing and eating other animals are called predators. The animals they target—their prey—defend themselves in ways that can end up being deadly. Other animals can be deadly because of completely different aspects of their behavior. For example, parasites feed on other living things without immediately killing them but can spread deadly diseases when they bite.

PREDATORS

Muscles, jaws, and claws
Many predators use brute strength and weaponry to attack and kill their prey.

Venomous bites
Venom-laced bites have mainly evolved to kill prey but are sometimes used in self-defense.

Traps
By setting a trap to catch prey, predators save energy in a chase or a fight.

Deceivers and tricksters
Some predators can pretend to be harmless objects and hide in ambush, or imitate food to attract prey.

Skills, tactics, and cunning
Super senses, brain power, and speed can all help a predator catch its prey.

DEFENDERS

Muscles, jaws, and claws
Strength and weaponry can sometimes turn a cornered defender into a deadly killer.

Stings and poisons
Painful stings and foul-tasting poisons have evolved to keep predators away but sometimes have deadly effects.

Deadly numbers
Strength in numbers is a powerful defense—and is sometimes used to help overcome prey.

PARASITES

Disease and destruction
Some animals carry diseases that can kill, while other animals may be destructive to habitats when they invade new regions.

1

MUSCLES, JAWS, AND CLAWS

A Siberian tiger's daggerlike canine teeth—the longest of any cat—are adapted to kill. When animals clash, size and strength can help them stay alive. Many wield physical weapons, such as teeth and claws, with lethal effects—both in predatory attacks and in self-defense.

GIANT SQUID
Architeuthis dux

Found in the darkness of the deep ocean, this lethal hunter is one of the biggest animals without a backbone. Its eight muscular arms and two tentacles—the longest of any squid—have suckers for catching prey. Once caught, the prey is torn apart with the squid's hooked beak.

Enormous eyes may **help** this squid **avoid** its **enemy**, sperm whales.

Muscles, jaws, and claws

DATA FILE

DANGER FACTOR
! ! ! !

SIZE: Up to 59 ft (18 m) long

RANGE: Worldwide in the deep ocean

DIET: Fish and other squid

GIANT PACIFIC
OCTOPUS
Enteroctopus dofleini

DATA FILE

 DANGER FACTOR

SIZE: Arm span up to 31.5 ft (9.6 m) long

 RANGE: Coastlines of the North Pacific Ocean

DIET: Crabs, lobsters, shrimp, clams, and fish

Found in cold ocean waters, this creature has the biggest arm span compared to other octopus species. It combines brain and brawn to grab anything tasty that comes within its massive reach. A trash pile next to its underwater lair contains the remains of its victims. It eats animals up to the size of small sharks and even the occasional seabird.

This octopus can squeeze through a hole the size of its beak—the only hard part of its body.

Muscles, jaws, and claws

PEACOCK
MANTIS SHRIMP
Odontodactylus scyllarus

This colorful crustacean hides at the bottom of coral reefs and packs a deadly punch. The peacock mantis shrimp holds a pair of solid clubs under the front of its body. When a crab wanders close, the shrimp swings the clubs with the speed of a bullet to hammer its victim's shell to pieces. It has the strength to smash the glass of an aquarium.

Prey-smashing clubs are carried on the second pair of legs.

Peacock mantis shrimp, front view

Muscles, jaws, and claws

Peacock mantis shrimp have even **better vision than humans.**

DATA FILE

DANGER FACTOR
! ! !

SIZE: 2–7 in (5–17 cm) long

RANGE: Eastern Africa to Japan, Australia, and southwestern Pacific

DIET: Crabs, snails, and fish

Mantis shrimp threaten rivals and enemies by flashing colorful paddles on their antennae.

Like other crustaceans, the mantis shrimp is covered in a hard armorlike exoskeleton.

Muscles, jaws, and claws

CAMEL SPIDER

Solifugae

This eight-legged desert hunter is not venomous, but it makes up for this by having enormous jaws. After chasing down or ambushing prey, a camel spider uses its jaws like pincers to rip the victim apart while it is still struggling—even snapping through tiny bones.

Muscles, jaws, and claws

A camel spider can move at the speed of **10 mph (16 km/h)**.

GREAT WHITE
SHARK
Carcharodon carcharias

DATA FILE

 DANGER FACTOR

 SIZE: 11–20 ft
(3.5–6 m) long

 RANGE: Oceans worldwide,
except cold polar waters

 DIET: Fish, marine mammals,
seabirds, squid, and
crustaceans

Great white shark, side view

One of the ocean's biggest top predators, the great white shark has the power to kill mammals the size of elephant seals and baby whales. This shark disables its biggest prey with a huge bite, then it may wait for the victim to bleed to death before devouring it.

Sawlike teeth and powerful jaws help this shark carve through bone and blubber.

Muscles, jaws, and claws

BULL SHARK

Carcharhinus leucas

DATA FILE

 DANGER FACTOR

SIZE: Up to 11.2 ft (3.4 m) long

RANGE: Coastal waters of tropics worldwide; sometimes in rivers

DIET: Other fish, invertebrates, and carrion

Unusually for sharks, this underwater predator can survive in fresh water and occasionally wanders up the rivers, far from the salty ocean. Here it continues to hunt, even when close to the riverbank and near people. This behavior, along with its massive jaws and big appetite, makes it a potentially dangerous shark.

Bull shark, side view

The bull shark has tiny eyes and poor eyesight, so it mainly relies on its other senses—such as smell—to locate prey.

Muscles, jaws, and claws

ARAPAIMA

Arapaima

The predatory arapaima is one of the biggest of all freshwater fish. It is found in the murky flooded waters of the Amazon river and uses a special lung to breathe air. Every 10 minutes, it rises to the surface to take a gulp or, if it is hungry, to grab an unsuspecting bird.

The arapaima raises its young in **nest holes** made **in the river bed**.

DATA FILE

 DANGER FACTOR

 SIZE: Up to 14.7 ft (4.5 m) long

 RANGE: Rivers of the Amazon basin

 DIET: Wide variety of animals

Muscles, jaws, and claws

VIPERFISH
Chauliodus

The viperfish has the longest teeth in proportion to its head than any other fish. In its dark ocean habitat, this ferocious predator uses its impressive teeth to ensure that its prey doesn't escape. The long fangs close around a struggling target like a cage, trapping the victim before it is swallowed whole.

DATA FILE

 DANGER FACTOR

 SIZE: 5.9–13.7 in (15–35 cm) long, depending on species

 RANGE: Deep ocean worldwide

 DIET: Other fish, crustaceans, and arrow worms

The viperfish has light-producing organs, possibly to help attract prey.

The viperfish can **swallow prey** that reaches **63 percent** of its **body length**.

Muscles, jaws, and claws

SALTWATER CROCODILE
Crocodylus porosus

No other reptile grows as big as the saltwater crocodile. It lives along coastlines, and unlike other crocodiles, regularly swims out to sea. Victims are ambushed at the water's edge, then dragged beneath the surface and drowned as the reptile spins around and around in a so-called "death roll." This large predator then feasts on the victim, tearing up large chunks.

The biggest of these crocodiles can **weigh** more than **2,200 lb** (1 tonne).

Muscles, jaws, and claws

GREEN
ANACONDA
Eunectes murinus

Weighing up to 154 lb (70 kg), the green anaconda is the world's heaviest snake. It is slow and cumbersome on land but more agile in water, where it watches for prey with its eyes just above the surface. This formidable predator kills by constriction, tightening its coils around its victim and squeezing so hard that it stops its prey's heart from pumping blood.

DATA FILE

DANGER FACTOR
! ! ! ! !

SIZE: Up to 17.3 ft (5.3 m) long

RANGE: Swamps of tropical South America

DIET: Animals up to the size of deer

Muscles, jaws, and claws

PERENTIE
Varanus giganteus

Perentie, side view

Australia's largest lizard has a tail that is longer than the length of its head and body. The perentie uses its tail to swipe at an attacker—with a force that is said to be strong enough to break a dog's leg. Although it prefers smaller prey, it can overpower anything up to the size of a small kangaroo using its sharp teeth and claws.

A threatened perentie opens its mouth wide to ward off attackers.

DATA FILE

DANGER FACTOR
❗❗❗ ● ●

SIZE: Up to 6.5 ft (2 m) long, head to tail

RANGE: Deserts of western and central Australia

DIET: Animals, eggs, and carrion

KOMODO DRAGON
Varanus komodoensis

The world's biggest lizard, the Komodo dragon is at the top of its food chain on the tropical island of Komodo, Indonesia. An adult dragon ambushes prey as big as deer. It attacks with a slashing bite and sharp claws that leave prey badly wounded. Most victims die quickly from shock or blood loss. The reptile then gorges on meat and bones, and later regurgitates the indigestible hair and horns in a slimy pellet.

Komodo dragons can smell the oils from decomposing carcasses over long distances.

Komodo dragon, side view

The saliva is laced with small amounts of venom.

Muscles, jaws, and claws

The **biggest** Komodo dragons sometimes **prey on smaller ones**.

DATA FILE

DANGER FACTOR
! ! ! ! !

SIZE: Up to 9.8 ft (3 m) long, from head to tail

RANGE: Komodo, and other nearby islands in Indonesia

DIET: Deer, reptiles, pigs, rodents, monkeys, eggs, insects, and carrion

Muscles, jaws, and claws

SOUTHERN CASSOWARY

Casuarius casuarius

Found in rainforests, this flightless bird weighs up to 128 lb (58 kg) and is one of the largest birds in the world. It prefers to stay hidden in the undergrowth, but if cornered the southern cassowary can kick out with both feet at once, and its long, sharp claws (on its inner toes) can rip open an attacker's belly.

Southern cassowary, side view

DATA FILE

DANGER FACTOR

SIZE: 39–67 in (100–170 cm) tall

RANGE: New Guinea and northeastern Australia

DIET: Mainly fallen fruit; also fungi, small animals, and sometimes carrion

The cassowary's daggerlike claws are lethal.

Muscles, jaws, and claws

SECRETARYBIRD
Sagittarius serpentarius

The secretarybird gets its name from the crest of black feathers on its head, which resemble the quill pens that secretaries once used. This long-legged relative of hawks and eagles kills its prey by stamping on them with its thick feet. Anything small enough is then swallowed whole, while larger prey is held down by the toes and torn apart with its hooked bill.

By kicking with its feet, the secretarybird can even overcome venomous snakes, such as adders and cobras.

DATA FILE

DANGER FACTOR

SIZE: Up to 47 in (120 cm) tall

RANGE: Grasslands in Africa, south of the Sahara desert

DIET: Grasshoppers and beetles; also frogs, reptiles, and small mammals

Muscles, jaws, and claws

OSPREY
Pandion haliaetus

Fish can be slippery prey, but the osprey is superbly adapted for catching them. It plunges into the water from heights of 98 ft (30 m) and uses its long, bare legs to reach below the surface. Spiny pads on its feet and its long talons help it to grip a fish.

DATA FILE

 DANGER FACTOR
❗ ❗ ❗ ⚪ ⚪

 SIZE: 21.6–22.8 in (55–58 cm) long

 RANGE: Nearly worldwide; found near shallow water

 DIET: Fish

The osprey's nose valves **close during** a **dive** to stop water entering its nostrils.

Muscles, jaws, and claws

HARPY EAGLE
Harpia harpyja

The harpy is one of several kinds of eagles with a head crest.

The harpy eagle is one of the largest raptors in the world. Up to one-third of prey taken by this huge rainforest eagle are slow-moving sloths—but it can also catch speedy monkeys. Most sloth prey are caught when they climb into treetops—this hunter easily spots them and makes its swooping attack.

DATA FILE

DANGER FACTOR

SIZE: 35–41.3 in (89–105 cm) long

RANGE: Tropical forests of Central and South America

DIET: Sloths, monkeys, reptiles, and other large animals

Muscles, jaws, and claws

TASMANIAN
DEVIL
Sarcophilus harrisii

For its size, the Tasmanian devil has the **strongest bite** of **any mammal**.

This marsupial can be easily identified by its eerie screeches late at night. Despite its short legs, the Tasmanian devil can roam up to 6 miles (9 km) to eat. It relishes a carcass as much as fresh meat. A large group of devils will squabble noisily over a dead animal, crunching its bones with amazingly strong jaws.

When agitated, the Tasmanian devil's ears can turn bright red.

DATA FILE

DANGER FACTOR
❗ ❗ ❗ ⬤ ⬤

SIZE: Up to 36 in (91 cm) long, head to tail

RANGE: Forests and grassy woodlands of Tasmania

DIET: Possums, wombats, and carrion

Muscles, jaws, and claws

SIBERIAN
TIGER
Panthera tigris altaica

The biggest kinds of living cats are tigers that live in the cold, snowy forests of Asia. The Siberian tiger is an expert at creeping close to its prey before swiping the victim to the ground with its sharp claws. The biggest deer are strangled with a bite to the throat.

DATA FILE

DANGER FACTOR
! ! ! ! !

SIZE: Up to 157 in (399 cm) long, head to tail

RANGE: Russian Far East and northeastern China

DIET: Mainly deer and wild pigs

Muscles, jaws, and claws

CLOUDED LEOPARD
Neofelis

Clouded leopard, side view

Muscles, jaws, and claws

This predator has the longest canine teeth, in proportion to its head, of any living cat—making the clouded leopard something like a modern version of a prehistoric saber-toothed cat. The massive muscles in its mouth stretch right over the back of its skull, helping this deadly predator clamp down on prey with a formidable killing bite.

DATA FILE

DANGER FACTOR
❗ ❗ ❗ ❗ ⬤

SIZE: Up to 76 in (192 cm) long, from head to tail

RANGE: Tropical forests of Southeast Asia

DIET: Porcupines, pigs, small deer, primates, birds, and fish

WOLVERINE
Gulo gulo

A wolverine kills with a bite to the head or neck.

Wolverine, side view

The wolverine looks like a small bear but is really the biggest member of the weasel family. Although it usually eats from carcasses left by speedier wolves, when animals are hindered by thick snow, it can bring down prey as big as reindeer.

DATA FILE

DANGER FACTOR
! ! ! !

SIZE: 26–41 in (65–105 cm) long, head and body

RANGE: Coniferous forests and tundra around the Northern Hemisphere

DIET: Carrion, rodents, rabbits, deer, birds, and eggs

Muscles, jaws, and claws

LEOPARD SEAL

Hydrurga leptonyx

Leopard seal, side view

In freezing Antarctica, carnivorous leopard seals hunt anything they can overpower—including other seals. Their tactics change through the seasons. When penguins are breeding during the summer, the seals lurk between the ice floes to catch and devour the birds that are fishing to feed their chicks.

Muscles, jaws, and claws

DATA FILE

 DANGER FACTOR

 SIZE: 7.8–11.1 ft (2.4–3.4 m) long

 RANGE: Icepacks around Antarctica

 DIET: Fish, penguins, squid, and other ocean animals

SPERM WHALE

Physeter macrocephalus

All the sperm whale's teeth are in the narrow lower jaw.

Many giant whales feed by straining small ocean plankton, but the sperm whale prefers meatier prey. It is the biggest living animal with teeth, used for biting larger prey. This deep-sea hunter dives down to 1.2 miles (2 km) below the ocean surface, holding its breath for more than an hour, in search of its favorite food—deep-sea squid.

DATA FILE

 DANGER FACTOR
❗ ❗ ❗ ❗ ⚫

 SIZE: 34.1–63 ft (10.4–19.2 m) long

 RANGE: Oceans worldwide

 DIET: Squid and fish

Muscles, jaws, and claws

2

VENOMOUS BITES

Strong bites can inflict serious injury, but bites that carry venom can be especially dangerous. Each venom is a cocktail of harmful substances. Some venoms can cripple the muscles, while others can shut down vital organs, but all are effective in overpowering prey or driving away enemies.

BLUE-RINGED
OCTOPUS
Hapalochlaena

Many kinds of octopus in the ocean rely on size and brute strength, but this small octopus relies on particularly strong venom for defense and to kill prey. Before it bites, the bright blue rings on its body intensify as a warning. It can be found on coastlines and coral reefs. One octopus carries enough venom to kill 26 people.

DATA FILE

DANGER FACTOR
! ! ! ! !

SIZE: 4.7–8.6 in (12–22 cm) long, depending on species

RANGE: Tropical Asia, Japan, New Guinea, and Australia

DIET: Crabs, shrimp, and other crustaceans

Venomous bites

ARROW WORM
Chaetognatha

Arrow worms live among the tiny animals that drift in ocean water. They dart through the water like little arrows and feed by gulping particles in the seawater. Armed with clawlike jaws, they sometimes grab bigger prey—and even paralyze it with venom.

DATA FILE

 DANGER FACTOR

 SIZE: 0.07–4.7 in (2–120 mm) long, depending on species

 RANGE: Worldwide, from shallows to deep sea

 DIET: Microscopic food particles; also crustaceans and tiny fish

Venomous bites

YELLOW-LEGGED
GIANT CENTIPEDE

Scolopendra gigantea

Its **bite** can **kill a mouse** in **30 seconds**.

This deadly predator dwells in tropical forests. It is the world's largest centipede and can grow to the length of a small snake. Its long antennae help it detect prey through touch and scent. Like all centipedes, it has venomous fangs that are used to kill prey, but this giant can use them to kill much larger prey, such as mice and birds. It can even hunt bats on the ceilings of caves, using its strong legs to crawl up the walls and attack with a deadly bite.

Venomous bites

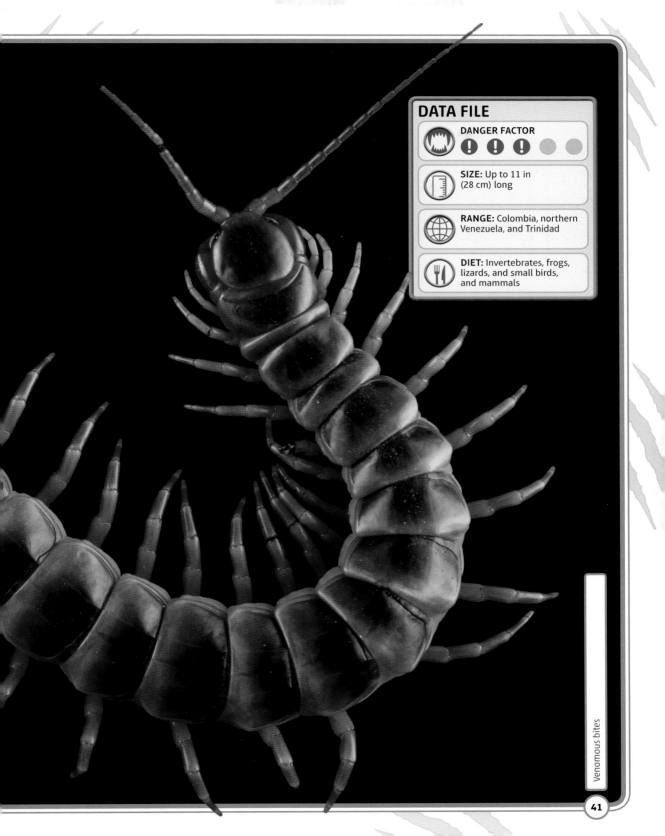

DATA FILE

DANGER FACTOR
❗ ❗ ❗

SIZE: Up to 11 in (28 cm) long

RANGE: Colombia, northern Venezuela, and Trinidad

DIET: Invertebrates, frogs, lizards, and small birds, and mammals

Venomous bites

SYDNEY FUNNEL-WEB
SPIDER
Atrax robustus

Found mainly in forests, the funnel-web spider is so-called because it lurks in funnel-like burrows to wait for passing prey. Triplines of silk extend from the burrow's entrance, so that when prey stumble across them, the spider is alerted. The Sydney funnel-web found in Australia is the deadliest of the bunch, and its venom is strong enough to kill a human.

DATA FILE

DANGER FACTOR
❗ ❗ ❗ ❗ ⬤

SIZE: 0.5–1.3 in (1.5–3.5 cm) long, head and body

RANGE: Southeastern Australia

DIET: Insects, cockroaches, small lizards, and other small animals

An aggressive male funnel-web rears up when it is threatened to expose its enormous fangs.

Funnel-webs often **fall** into garden **swimming pools**, where they **survive** for hours.

Venomous bites

BROWN RECLUSE
SPIDER
Loxosceles reclusa

Living near humans provides this spider with its perfect home—the nooks and crannies in a shed, garage, or house. The recluse spider goes wandering at night in search of insect prey. When it bites in self-defense, it can produce a wound that sometimes turns into a big open sore.

DATA FILE

DANGER FACTOR
! ! ! !

SIZE: 0.2–0.7 in (0.5–2 cm) long, head and body

RANGE: Various habitats in southern US

DIET: Insects

Venomous bites

REDBACK SPIDER
Latrodectus hasselti

Female redback spiders usually **eat** the **males** during **mating**.

Females have a red stripe on their back and a red hourglass shape underneath.

Native to dry forests and deserts, this infamous spider likes to build its tangled web in the shelter of buildings. It uses its venom to paralyze small prey, but also attacks in self-defense if a careless hand gets too close. Bigger females inject more venom than the males. Their painful bites can cause sickness and headaches in humans.

DATA FILE

DANGER FACTOR

SIZE: Male body 0.11–0.15 in (3–4 mm) long, female body up to 0.4 in (10 mm)

RANGE: Australia, introduced to Asia

DIET: Mainly insects; also woodlice, other spiders, and lizards

Venomous bites

ROBBER FLY

Asilidae

DATA FILE

DANGER FACTOR
!! ! ● ● ●

SIZE: 0.1–2.3 in (0.5–6 cm) long, wingspan up to 3.1 in (8 cm)

RANGE: Worldwide, except for Hawaii and Antarctica

DIET: Other flies, wasps, beetles, and butterflies

The falcon of the insect world, this fly scans for flying insects from a perch and then attacks. Found in grasslands and deserts, it grabs a target, such as a grasshopper, in midair with its strong bristly legs. The robber fly then stabs into its prey's neck, eyes, or other soft parts using its pointed mouthparts.

Most robber flies have a long, tapering abdomen, but in some species it is short and squat to mimic bees.

Venomous bites

GILA MONSTER

Heloderma suspectum

Unlike venomous snakes, which bite quickly and wait for their poison to take effect, the gila monster—one of only two kinds of venomous lizard—likes to make sure its poison will work. It keeps a tight hold on its victim and keeps chewing so that even more venom seeps into the wound.

Gila monster, top view

The gila monster, the largest lizard in the US, has tiny beadlike scales on its body.

Venomous bites

46

GABOON VIPER
Bitis gabonica

The viper's eyes can move more than those of other snakes, helping it to scan its surroundings.

The gaboon viper's body pattern gives it perfect camouflage against the leaf litter of a forest floor.

Fangs can grow up to 1.9 in (5 cm) long

This big snake breaks all the records. It is the world's heaviest venomous snake, has the longest fangs, and produces the most venom. Although less aggressive than other kinds of vipers, it doesn't let go when it bites and has the strength to overpower a small deer.

Venomous bites

SAW-SCALED VIPER
Echis carinatus

The saw-scaled viper can **climb** into **trees** to **attack nestling birds**.

By living in close proximity to people, the saw-scaled viper may be responsible for more human fatalities than any other reptile. Its venom is not particularly strong, but an earth-colored body and nocturnal habits mean it is not easily seen—until it bites.

Venomous bites

DATA FILE

DANGER FACTOR

SIZE: 20–29 in (50–73 cm) long

RANGE: Deserts and dry shrubland in the Middle East and India

DIET: Rodents, lizards, frogs, invertebrates, and nestling birds

BLACK MAMBA
Dendroaspis polylepis

DATA FILE

 DANGER FACTOR
!!!!!

 SIZE: 98–167 in (250–425 cm) long

 RANGE: Wooded savanna and rocky hillsides in Africa

DIET: Small mammals and birds

The black lining of this reptile's mouth gives it its name.

Black mamba, side view

This snake's threat display should be enough to keep anyone away. It rears its coffin-shaped head high from the ground, then hisses and gapes a black-lined mouth. If that doesn't work, the black mamba—possibly the world's fastest snake—strikes many times in quick succession to inject its paralyzing venom.

Venomous bites

BOOMSLANG
Dispholidus typus

The big eyes of the tree-living boomslang help it to spot prey high among the branches. Unlike many other dangerously venomous snakes, its fangs are hidden at the back of its mouth—but they are no less deadly when it bites. The effects of its venom may be delayed, but over a few hours cause potentially fatal internal bleeding.

DATA FILE

 DANGER FACTOR

 SIZE: Up to 6.5 ft (2 m) long

 RANGE: Forests and open woodland in Africa

 DIET: Small mammals, birds, and reptiles

The boomslang has an egg-shaped head with jaws that can open to 170 degrees.

Venomous bites

50

INLAND
TAIPAN
Oxyuranus microlepidotus

The inland taipan is rarely seen because it lives in the remote outback of Australia. But this shy snake is a record-breaker—it has the deadliest venom of any snake tested so far. Its bite contains a chemical that speeds the spread of the venom—a small animal is dead even before the snake lets go.

One drop of the inland taipan's venom is enough to **kill 100 humans**.

The snake raises its body into an S-shape when it feels threatened.

Venomous bites

KING
COBRA
Ophiophagus hannah

The world's longest venomous snake, the king cobra has very particular tastes—it only eats other snakes. In defense, the king cobra (especially a mother guarding a nest of eggs) puts on an impressive display in the face of any attacker. It raises its head 5 ft (1.5 m) from the ground and, instead of hissing, growls from the depths of its throat.

Venomous bites

King cobra, side view

DATA FILE

DANGER FACTOR
! ! ! !

SIZE: Up to 13 ft (4 m) long

RANGE: Woodlands of tropical Asia

DIET: Other snakes

A king cobra's **bite** contains enough **venom** to **kill** an **Asian elephant**.

NORTHERN SHORT-TAILED
SHREW
Blarina brevicauda

If a **human** is **bitten** by a shrew, it can be **painful** for **days**.

Venomous bites

Shrews live frantic lives and have big appetites—they are forever on the hunt for food. Some shrews have venomous bites. The strong venom of a short-tailed shrew not only helps to overpower bigger prey, but also keeps victims paralyzed and fresh. Once caught, the prey is stored in a "living pantry" to eat later.

DATA FILE

 DANGER FACTOR
❗ ❗ ⬤ ⬤ ⬤

 SIZE: 3.5–5.3 in (9–13.5 cm) long

 RANGE: Grasslands and woodlands in North America

 DIET: Animals up to the size of frogs, snakes, and small birds

SLOW LORIS
Nycticebus

DATA FILE

 DANGER FACTOR
 ❗ ❗ ⚫ ⚫ ⚫

 SIZE: 7.8–14.9 in (20–38 cm) long

RANGE: Rainforests in Southeast Asia

 DIET: Fruits, leaves, tree gum, and small animals

This slow-moving relative of lemurs looks cuddly and harmless, but it hides a remarkable defense—it is the only venomous primate. By licking a gland near its elbow, the slow loris mixes a special oil with its saliva to produce a toxic mixture—strong enough to kill a small animal with a bite.

In extreme cases, its **venom** causes an **allergic reaction** in humans.

Venomous bites

3 STINGS AND POISONS

Painful stings or poisons that cause sickness are
a good defense against attackers—and some
stingers, such as those carried on the tentacles
of a sea wasp, are able to kill prey, too.

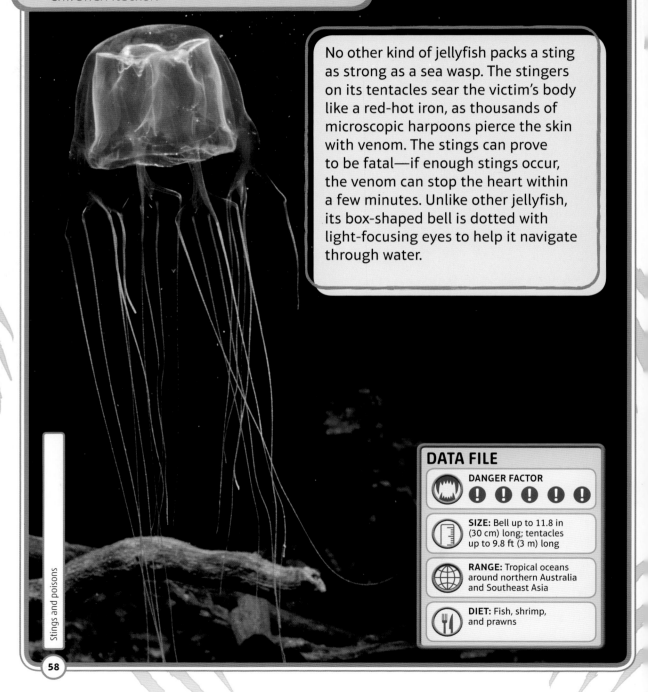

SEA WASP
Chironex fleckeri

No other kind of jellyfish packs a sting as strong as a sea wasp. The stingers on its tentacles sear the victim's body like a red-hot iron, as thousands of microscopic harpoons pierce the skin with venom. The stings can prove to be fatal—if enough stings occur, the venom can stop the heart within a few minutes. Unlike other jellyfish, its box-shaped bell is dotted with light-focusing eyes to help it navigate through water.

DATA FILE

DANGER FACTOR
! ! ! ! !

SIZE: Bell up to 11.8 in (30 cm) long; tentacles up to 9.8 ft (3 m) long

RANGE: Tropical oceans around northern Australia and Southeast Asia

DIET: Fish, shrimp, and prawns

Stings and poisons

BEARDED FIREWORM
Hermodice carunculata

DATA FILE

DANGER FACTOR

SIZE: Up to 11.8 in (30 cm) long

RANGE: Caribbean, western Africa, and the Mediterranean sea

DIET: Mainly corals and colonial anemones

Most worms prefer to stay hidden from their predators. But the seashore-living bearded fireworm has a defense that lets it munch on coral in plain view of likely predators. Its body is covered in glassy bristles that snap off at the slightest touch to pour painful, numbing venom into its attacker's skin.

Stings and poisons

PURPLE CONE
SNAIL
Conus purpurascens

A slow snail with a taste for meat needs a clever skill to catch fast-moving prey. The purple cone snail has a particularly deadly technique—it shoots anything that comes close with a venom-spiked harpoon. The victim is killed within seconds, and then funneled into the snail's enormous mouth.

CALIFORNIA SEA
HARE
Aplysia californica

This giant sea slug collects poisonous chemicals by munching on red seaweed. It can store enough poison to kill an animal the size of a mouse. Only a hard-shelled lobster might not be deterred by the poison. But the sea hare uses another defense tactic—it squirts an inky fluid that bewilders the attacker's senses.

A tubelike siphon breathes in water for oxygen, but can also taste the presence of nearby prey.

DATA FILE

DANGER FACTOR ! ! ! ! !

SIZE: Shell up to 27.5 in (70 cm) long

RANGE: Pacific coasts of Galápagos Islands and Mexico to Peru

DIET: Worms, fish, and other snails

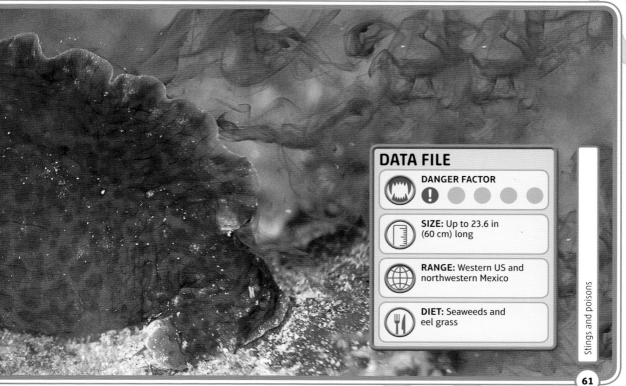

DATA FILE

DANGER FACTOR !

SIZE: Up to 23.6 in (60 cm) long

RANGE: Western US and northwestern Mexico

DIET: Seaweeds and eel grass

Stings and poisons

DISCO CLAM
Ctenoides ales

This ocean clam has a fleshy lip around its shell. The lip catches and reflects light when it moves up and down, producing flashes of light in a dazzling display—just like a disco light. Research suggests that clams flash faster when food or danger are near. This could be to attract plankton prey or warn predators that their flesh contains poisonous sulfuric acid.

DATA FILE

 DANGER FACTOR

 SIZE: Up to 3.5 in (9 cm) in diameter

 RANGE: Tropical oceans of Southeast Asia

 DIET: Small organisms floating in plankton

FLAMBOYANT CUTTLEFISH
Metasepia pfefferi

Flamboyant cuttlefish, side view

This little cuttlefish is found in tropical oceans. It has flamboyant colors to warn that its flesh contains deadly poison. This sly predator walks along the ocean floor to stalk its prey, then shoots a dartlike pair of tentacles to grab it when within range.

DATA FILE

DANGER FACTOR

SIZE: Body up to 3 in (8 cm) long

RANGE: Southeast Asia, New Guinea, and Australia

DIET: Small fish, shrimp, and prawns

Stings and poisons

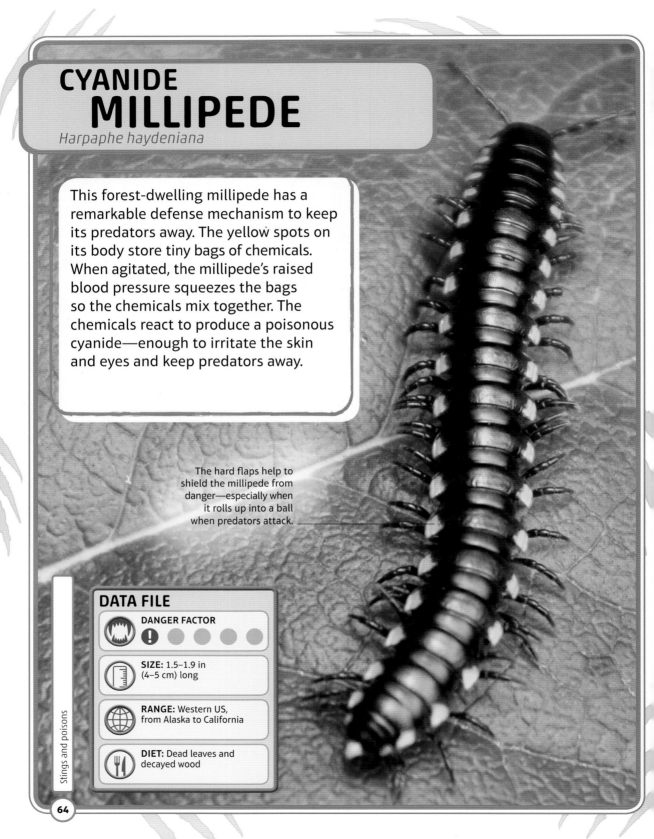

CYANIDE MILLIPEDE
Harpaphe haydeniana

This forest-dwelling millipede has a remarkable defense mechanism to keep its predators away. The yellow spots on its body store tiny bags of chemicals. When agitated, the millipede's raised blood pressure squeezes the bags so the chemicals mix together. The chemicals react to produce a poisonous cyanide—enough to irritate the skin and eyes and keep predators away.

The hard flaps help to shield the millipede from danger—especially when it rolls up into a ball when predators attack.

DATA FILE

DANGER FACTOR
!

SIZE: 1.5–1.9 in (4–5 cm) long

RANGE: Western US, from Alaska to California

DIET: Dead leaves and decayed wood

Stings and poisons

DEATHSTALKER
Leiurus quinquestriatus

Found in stony deserts, the deathstalker defends itself by stabbing with the stinger on its tail. It's not the biggest type of scorpion, but its venom is dangerous for humans. It is responsible for 85 percent of scorpion attacks on humans—and 90 percent of human deaths from scorpions.

Venom is made inside a sac at the end of the deathstalker's tail, just behind its curved, needle-sharp stinger.

DATA FILE

DANGER FACTOR

SIZE: 3.1–4.3 in (80–110 mm) long

RANGE: Northern Africa, Arabia, and the Middle East

DIET: Insects, centipedes, spiders, and other scorpions

A **sting** from this scorpion can cause **heart failure**.

Stings and poisons

SPANISH FLY
Lytta vesicatoria

DATA FILE

DANGER FACTOR
! ! !

SIZE: 0.7 in (2 cm) long

RANGE: Europe and northern and central Asia

DIET: Leaves of trees, such as lilac and ash

Wing cases have a metallic emerald-green sheen.

This woodland insect is not a fly, but a kind of beetle. It gets its name from the poisonous chemical (also called "Spanish fly") that comes from the males' body in a milky liquid. The bitter taste and blistering effects of the poison deter insect-eaters and can lead to internal bleeding and organ failure in humans.

Stings and poisons

RATTLEBOX MOTH
CATERPILLAR
Utetheisa ornatrix

The rattlebox moth is named after the *Crotalaria*, or rattlebox, plant because it eats the plant and stores its poison. When these caterpillars change into moths, the poison is passed on, so both caterpillars and adults are protected from predators.

Caterpillars **eating** rattlebox **seeds** get **five times** as much **poison** as eating **leaves**.

DATA FILE

DANGER FACTOR
❗ ❗ ⬤ ⬤ ⬤

SIZE: Caterpillars 1.1–1.5 in (30–40 mm) long

RANGE: Southern Canada to Chile and Argentina

DIET: Caterpillars eat leaves and seeds of rattlebox plants

Stings and poisons

PUSS MOTH
CATERPILLAR
Megalopyge opercularis

The hairs on the puss moth caterpillar make it look like a soft Persian cat. Even after turning into a moth, it retains its silky coat. But this cuddly-looking caterpillar is one of the most dangerous. Its coat contains venomous spines, which can sting and feel as painful as breaking your arm.

DATA FILE

DANGER FACTOR

SIZE: Caterpillars up to 1.6 in (40 mm) long

RANGE: Open woodlands and forests of central and eastern US

DIET: Caterpillars eat leaves of oak and elm trees, and other plants

A **sting** can **cause vomiting, headaches**, and **breathing difficulty** in humans.

GIANT SILKWORM
MOTH CATERPILLAR
Lonomia obliqua

Tips of bristles on this caterpillar break when touched to inject venom into the skin.

DATA FILE

DANGER FACTOR
❗❗❗❗❗

SIZE: Caterpillars up to 2.2 in (55 mm) long

RANGE: Tropical forests and open woodlands of South America

DIET: Caterpillars eat leaves of a variety of plants

This most dangerous of caterpillars turns into a harmless moth. But before this transformation, it is truly deadly. The bristles that protect the caterpillars contain a venom that can cause internal bleeding and kidney failure in humans. These venom-injecting bristles are so well camouflaged that a carelessly placed hand could bring fatal results.

Stings and poisons

QUEEN ALEXANDRA'S
BIRDWING
Ornithoptera alexandrae

The biggest butterfly in the world, a Queen Alexandra's birdwing could be mistaken for a colorful bird as it flutters through its rainforest home. Even its giant caterpillar is brightly colored—a warning that it stores poisons, which it gets from eating a tropical vine. When the caterpillar transforms into a butterfly, the poisons stay in its body to protect the adult from predators, too.

The **poison** in this butterfly causes severe **vomiting** in an unknowing **predator**.

Queen Alexandra's birdwing caterpillar

This female birdwing
has dark brown wings
with yellow spots. Males
are slightly smaller with
black and blue wings.

DATA FILE

DANGER FACTOR
❗

SIZE: Wingspan up to
11 in (28 cm)

RANGE: Rainforests of
eastern New Guinea

DIET: Adults drink nectar;
caterpillars eat leaves of
Aristolochia vine

Stings and poisons

TARANTULA
HAWK
Pepsis

DATA FILE

DANGER FACTOR
! ! !

SIZE: 0.5–1.9 in (1.5–5 cm) long, depending on species

RANGE: Various habitats from North to South America

DIET: Spiders and nectar

The sting of this big wasp is said to be the most painful of any insect. The impact of the sting needs to be strong, because the female tarantula hawk uses it to paralyze tarantula spiders. When the spider is paralyzed, the wasp drags its motionless victim into a specially prepared burrow and lays an egg on top of it. When the egg hatches, the wasp's larva eats the spider alive.

Stings and poisons

MARICOPA HARVESTER
ANT
Pogonomyrmex maricopa

This ant spends its life harvesting seeds for food. When it comes to defending its nest, it uses the deadliest of insect venoms. Its sting is 20 times stronger than that of a honeybee, and it even sets off an alarm scent when under attack, which alerts other ants to come and help. Just a dozen stings can kill an animal the size of a rat.

DATA FILE

DANGER FACTOR

SIZE: Workers 0.2–0.3 in (6–7 mm) long

RANGE: Deserts of southern US and Mexico

DIET: Seeds and dead insects

The ant **bites down** with strong **jaws** while **stinging** an attacker.

As with other kinds of ants, the workers that defend a nest are female.

Stings and poisons

73

BULLET ANT
Paraponera clavata

This tiny but aggressive ant gets its name from its painful sting. The searing pain can last 24 hours and is said to be worse than the sting of any other insect. As part of an initiation ritual, rainforest Mawé tribal people fill a sleeve with bullet ants, and young men must wear the sleeve for 10 minutes to pass the test.

This bullet ant is attacking a small but equally aggressive army ant.

The bullet ant **lives** in **colonies** of **several thousand** individual ants.

Stings and poisons

FLOWER URCHIN

Toxopneustes pileolus

This sea urchin looks like a pretty bouquet of flowers, but danger lurks inside each pink bloom in the form of a sharp, venomous fang. If a careless diver touches the urchin, the fangs can break off in the skin and pump in venom for hours at a time.

The **venom** causes severe **pain and paralysis**—which could **drown** a human **diver**.

Stings and poisons

BLUE-SPOTTED
RIBBONTAIL STINGRAY

Taeniura lymma

This deadly creature has a serious sting in its tail, which has two venomous spines on top that are in the perfect position to defend a fish that spends its life on the sea bottom. While the stingray nuzzles in the sand for buried shellfish, a flick of the tail can sting any attacker that comes too close.

DATA FILE

DANGER FACTOR

SIZE: Up to 29.5 in (75 cm) long

RANGE: Reefs of eastern Africa, tropical Asia, and Australia

DIET: Mainly worms and mollusks

The **tail** spines of the ribbontail stingray can be **2.7 in (7 cm)** long.

STRIPED EEL CATFISH
Plotosus lineatus

Striped eel catfish, front view

The striped eel catfish is one of the few types of catfish found on coral reefs. Youngsters gather for safety in tight bunches and move like a single giant animal. But each individual also has fins with venomous saw-edged spines that can jab into the skin of a predator to cause a painful injury.

DATA FILE

DANGER FACTOR

SIZE: Up to 12.5 in (32 cm) long

RANGE: Eastern Africa, Asia, Australia, and western Pacific

DIET: Invertebrates and sometimes other fish

Stings and poisons

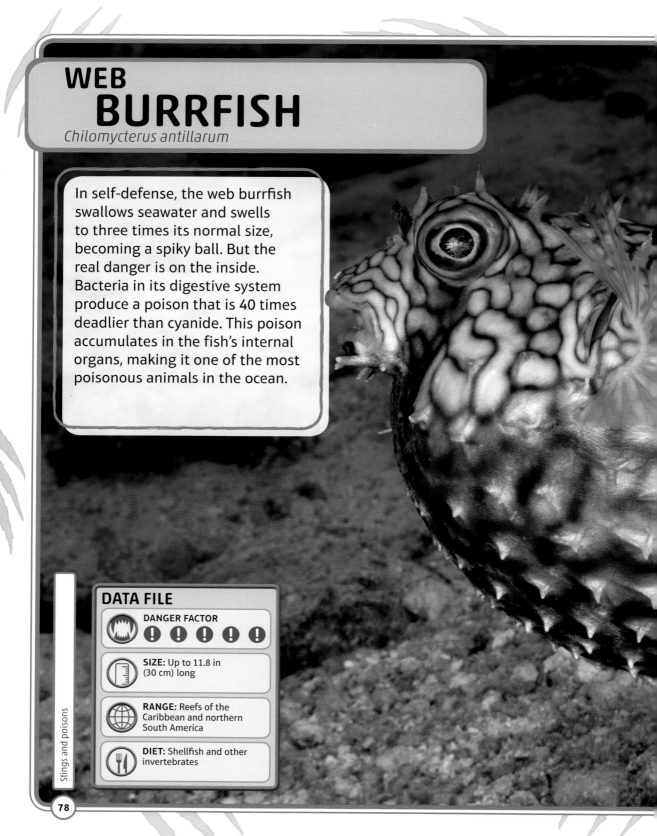

WEB BURRFISH
Chilomycterus antillarum

In self-defense, the web burrfish swallows seawater and swells to three times its normal size, becoming a spiky ball. But the real danger is on the inside. Bacteria in its digestive system produce a poison that is 40 times deadlier than cyanide. This poison accumulates in the fish's internal organs, making it one of the most poisonous animals in the ocean.

DATA FILE

DANGER FACTOR
! ! ! ! !

SIZE: Up to 11.8 in (30 cm) long

RANGE: Reefs of the Caribbean and northern South America

DIET: Shellfish and other invertebrates

Stings and poisons

This fish's **poison paralyzes** muscles, so it can stop **lungs** from working.

REEF STONEFISH
Synanceia verrucosa

The ocean's expert at camouflage looks like nothing more than a lump of rock. But this rock-resembling fish has 13 venomous spines on its back. These spines are deadly stingers, injecting a venom that could be fatal. The reef stonefish mainly uses its venom to fend off predators.

DATA FILE

 DANGER FACTOR

SIZE: Up to 15.7 in (40 cm) long

RANGE: From East Africa to Asia and Australia

DIET: Fish and crustaceans

ROUGH-SKINNED NEWT

Taricha granulosa

DANGER FACTOR

SIZE: Up to 8.6 in (22 cm) long, from head to tail

RANGE: Eastern North America, from Alaska to California

DIET: Insects, leeches, tadpoles, snails, and worms

Glands on the back of this forest-dwelling newt produce the same kind of deadly poison as the poison frogs of South America. Predatory birds and mammals leave this newt alone—a fraction of a drop of its poison can kill a mouse in less than 10 minutes.

Poison glands are concentrated in the rough, warty skin along the newt's back.

The newt lifts its **head, legs, and tail** to **flash** a **yellow** underside when it's **threatened**.

Stings and poisons

81

FIRE
SALAMANDER
Salamandra salamandra

This deadly amphibian lives in forests with well-shaded streams. Just like a wasp, the striking yellow and black pattern on its body is a warning to stay away. When facing danger, the salamander dips its head to aim the poison glands behind its eyes. It then sprays its attacker with poison.

DATA FILE

DANGER FACTOR

SIZE: Up to 11 in (28 cm) long, head to tail

RANGE: Central and southern Europe

DIET: Invertebrates, such as snails, spiders, centipedes, and beetles

GOLDEN POISON
FROG
Phyllobates terribilis

DATA FILE

 DANGER FACTOR

 SIZE: 1.8 in (45–47 mm) long

 RANGE: Andes of western Colombia

 DIET: Invertebrates, such as beetles, mites, and ants

The poison is stored in skin glands, and the strongest poison is in the glands on the frog's back.

Despite its tiny size, the golden poison frog is considered one of the world's deadliest animals. This rainforest-dwelling amphibian produces enough poison to kill 10 humans. Native peoples of the South American rainforest smear this poison on their blowgun darts to hunt animals for their meat.

Stings and poisons

HOODED PITOHUI
Pitohui dichrous

The feathers and skin of the hooded pitohui contain the same toxins that are found in South American poison frogs. Each bird has a high-enough toxin level to kill several mice, but probably not enough to kill bigger predators. Instead, scientists believe that the poisons are used to repel parasites, such as mites and ticks.

DATA FILE

DANGER FACTOR

SIZE: Up to 9 in (22–23 cm) long

RANGE: Tropical rainforests in New Guinea

DIET: Mainly fruits; also certain insects and grass seeds

Stings and poisons

PLATYPUS
Ornithorhynchus anatinus

The platypus, an aquatic egg-laying mammal, uses its ducklike bill to detect prey. It may appear harmless, but on the males' ankles are sharp spurs. During breeding season, the spurs stab with a venom that is strong enough to paralyze small animals and cause excruciating pain in humans.

Platypus spur

DATA FILE

DANGER FACTOR
❗ ❗ ○ ○ ○

SIZE: Up to 25 in (63 cm) long, from head to tail; spurs 0.6 in (1.5 cm)

RANGE: Eastern Australia, including Tasmania

DIET: Small aquatic insect larvae, crustaceans, tadpoles, and fish

Stings and poisons

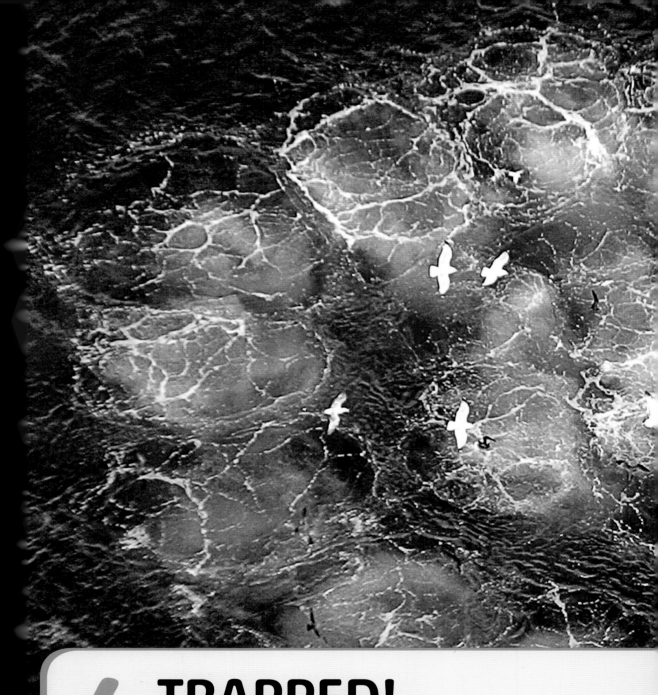

4 TRAPPED!

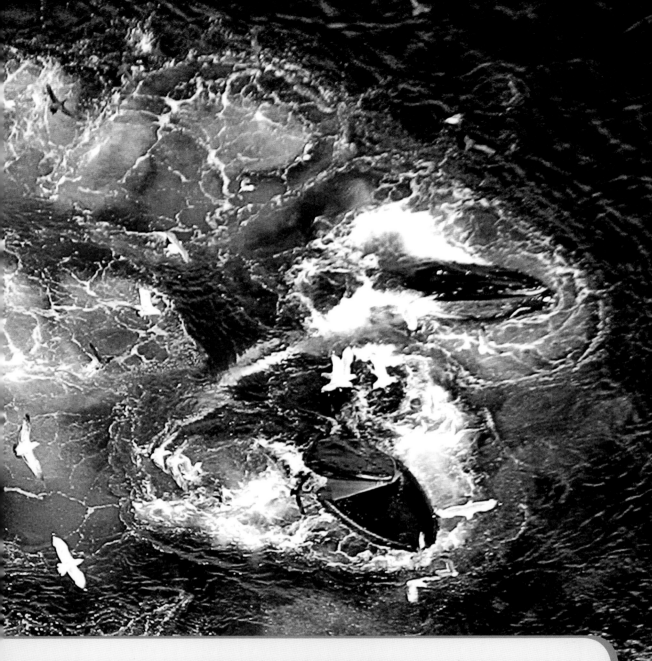

From the tiniest spiders to underwater giants, a huge variety of animals use different ways to trap prey. Humpback whales ensnare dense shoals of fish by blowing a circle of bubbles around them, then swallow them all with an upward gulp.

PREDATORY
TUNICATE
Megalodicopia hians

Anchored to the ocean bottom by a short stalk, the soft body of this animal has a remarkable way to get food. When tiny animals drift by, its broad hood snaps over them like a big mouth, just as the Venus flytrap plant catches insects on land. The hood stays closed until the meal is digested.

DATA FILE

 DANGER FACTOR
❗ ● ● ● ●

 SIZE: Up to 5.1 in (13 cm) in diameter

 RANGE: Deep waters of the Pacific Ocean

 DIET: Plankton

Trapped!

BROWN-LINED
RIBBON WORM
Baseodiscus hemprichii

Many kinds of worms end up being preyed upon by other animals—but for this extra-long oceanic ribbon worm, the tables are turned. This unlikely predator shoots the front part of its gut out through its mouth—just like turning the finger of a glove inside out. It then uses this muscular extension to grab prey.

DATA FILE

 DANGER FACTOR
❗ ❗ ⚪ ⚪ ⚪

 SIZE: Up to 26.2 ft (8 m) long

 RANGE: Shallow coastal waters of the Indian Ocean and western Pacific

 DIET: Other invertebrates

Trapped!

TRAPDOOR SPIDER
Ctenizidae

DATA FILE

 DANGER FACTOR
❗❗❗⚪⚪

SIZE: 0.3–1.1 in (1–3 cm) long, head and body

RANGE: Subtropical and tropical habitats virtually worldwide

DIET: Insects and other small invertebrates

No other hunter uses the element of surprise quite like a trapdoor spider. It makes a circular door from soil, which is tightly bound with webbing, then uses more silk for the hinge and to create triplines around the trap. The spider then waits beneath the closed door until an insect triggers the triplines. It then leaps out and catches its prey.

Trapped!

DARWIN'S BARK SPIDER
Caerostris darwini

The Darwin's bark spider is no bigger than your fingernail, but its web could span the width of a swimming pool—it has the biggest of all spider webs. It builds its trap across forest rivers to catch mayflies and other insects that like to fly over water. The silk used for this trap is the strongest material made by any animal.

DATA FILE

DANGER FACTOR
❗ ❗ ⬤ ⬤ ⬤

SIZE: Up to 0.8 in (22 mm) long, head and body

RANGE: Rainforests of Madagascar

DIET: Flying insects

Trapped!

OGRE-FACED
SPIDER
Deinopis

Like most spiders, the ogre-faced spider has eight eyes—but two of them are extra large. It needs big eyes for its special nighttime hunting technique. The spider holds its web by the legs just above the ground and uses it like a net to trap any small animal it sees crawling underneath. As the prey gets entangled in the net, the spider reaches down to bite.

DATA FILE

DANGER FACTOR
❗ ❗ ⬤ ⬤ ⬤

SIZE: 0.3–1.1 in (1–3 cm) long, head and body

RANGE: Forests and open woodlands throughout the tropics

DIET: Other invertebrates

This spider has **better nighttime vision** than a **cat**.

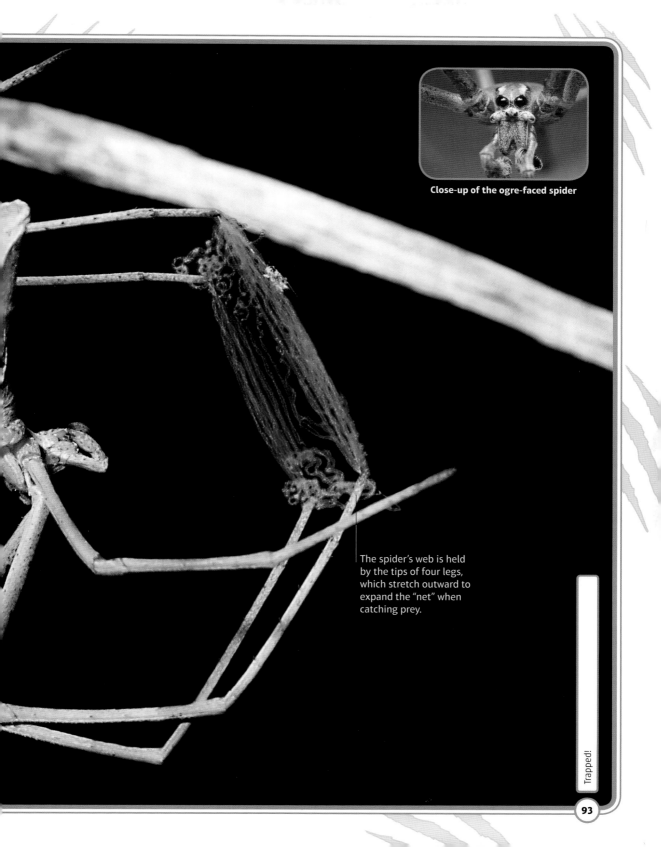

Close-up of the ogre-faced spider

The spider's web is held by the tips of four legs, which stretch outward to expand the "net" when catching prey.

ANTLION
LARVA
Myrmeleontidae

Before developing into a flying nectar-drinking insect, an antlion lives as a carnivorous larva with massive jaws for grabbing other insects. Some hide in leaf litter, but others dig pits in sand and wait at the bottom, part-buried, for any ants and other ground-dwelling insects to tumble inside.

GLOWING FUNGUS
GNAT LARVA
Arachnocampa

Some kinds of insects only feed when they are young larvae. And for a certain kind of gnat, the larvae are carnivorous. The luminous fungus gnat larva makes slimy threads that hang from a cave ceiling. The larva glows with light to attract flying insects. Once the prey gets caught by the sticky droplets, the larva crawls down to eat it.

Trapped!

DATA FILE

DANGER FACTOR

SIZE: Larva up to 0.8 in (2 cm) long

RANGE: Variety of habitats in warm regions worldwide

DIET: Larvae mainly eat other insects

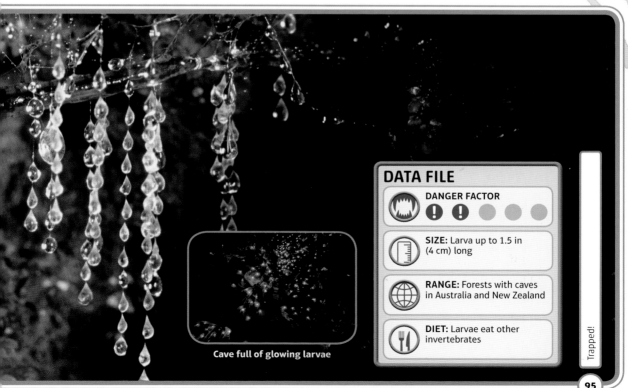

Cave full of glowing larvae

DATA FILE

DANGER FACTOR

SIZE: Larva up to 1.5 in (4 cm) long

RANGE: Forests with caves in Australia and New Zealand

DIET: Larvae eat other invertebrates

Trapped!

NEW ZEALAND
VELVET WORM
Peripatoides

This velvety-skinned animal looks like a worm with stubby legs, but it is actually distantly related to insects. It has a nozzle on each side of its mouth that squirts threads of sticky slime—both in defense and to catch any prey small enough to get trapped.

DATA FILE

DANGER FACTOR
❗ ● ● ● ●

SIZE: 0.7–3.1 in (2–8 cm) long

RANGE: Forests of New Zealand

DIET: Other smaller invertebrates

New Zealand velvet worm, front view

Trapped!

HUMPBACK WHALE

Megaptera novaeangliae

Groups of humpback whales come together and blow bubbles, forming a "bubble net," which forces shoals of fish into tight bunches and toward the surface. They then lunge upward with their mouths open to swallow their trapped prey.

DATA FILE

DANGER FACTOR

SIZE: 49.2–55.7 ft (15–17 m) long

RANGE: Oceans worldwide

DIET: Small fish and invertebrates of the ocean's plankton

Humpback whale, side view

Trapped!

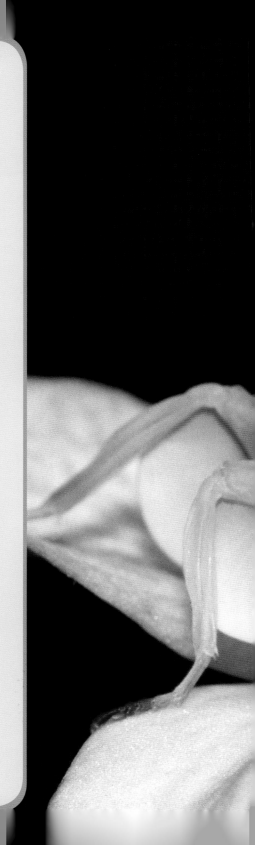

5
DECEIVERS AND TRICKSTERS

A predator that pretends to be something else can get an easy meal. A pink orchid mantis merges into a flower so it can grab any butterfly coming for a drink of nectar. But other tricksters mimic wiggling worms or use flashing lights to attract the unwary.

FLOWER CRAB SPIDER
Misumena vatia

DATA FILE

DANGER FACTOR

SIZE: 0.1–0.3 in (4–10 mm) long, head and body

RANGE: Woodlands and grasslands across the Northern Hemisphere

DIET: Insects that visit flowers

A flower is a good place to hide for an insect-hunter. This yellow spider finds perfect camouflage in yellow flowers, where it waits in ambush for visiting butterflies and bees who are in search of pollen. But if there are only white flowers around, it will wait there instead, as this spider can also change its color to white.

Crab spiders get their name from their legs, which spread out like a crab's.

Flower crab spider, front view

PORTIA
SPIDER
Portia

A portia spider looks like dead leaves so it can get close to prey without being noticed.

A spider that hunts other spiders needs to be especially smart to avoid becoming a victim. The portia spider could be the cleverest of the bunch. This jumping spider uses trial and error to find the best way to approach its victim—and may even rappel down on silken thread to attack the most aggressive targets from behind.

DATA FILE

DANGER FACTOR
❗ ❗ ● ● ●

SIZE: 0.1–0.4 in (4–12 mm) long

RANGE: Tropical Africa, Southeast Asia, and Australia

DIET: Mainly other spiders

Deceivers and tricksters

FEMME FATALE
LIGHTNING BUG
Photuris

Like all beetles, the front wings of this lightning bug are hardened to form a protective casing over its body when not flying.

The **light** comes from a **chemical reaction** in organs on the bug's **abdomen**.

Nocturnal fireflies are beetles that flash with light to attract a mate—but some types do it for more sinister reasons. The femme fatale lightning bug copies the flashing signal of other female fireflies to lure in unsuspecting males. Before the male realizes his mistake, he is seized and eaten.

DATA FILE

 DANGER FACTOR
❗ ❗ ● ● ●

 SIZE: 0.4–0.6 in (11–17 mm) long

 RANGE: Woodlands and grasslands of North America

 DIET: Fireflies

ORCHID
MANTIS
Hymenopus coronatus

DANGER FACTOR

❗ ❗ ⬤ ⬤ ⬤

SIZE: 1.1–2.3 in (3–6 cm) long

RANGE: Rainforests of Southeast Asia

DIET: Insects

Mantises are aggressive hunting insects that use their long front legs to snatch other insect prey. The other four legs are used for walking, but for the orchid mantis, they also serve another purpose—their wide pink lobes look like flower petals. This means that the tiny mantis can hide unseen in a flower—staying safe from predatory birds and catching butterflies that come to visit.

Deceivers and tricksters

MOTH BUTTERFLY
CATERPILLAR
Liphyra brassolis

Most caterpillars are vegetarian, but this one is a meat-eater. After hatching from its egg, it invades an ant nest to eat the ants' larvae. It probably produces a perfume to calm the ants so they don't fight back—giving it the chance to grow a protective leathery shield. The caterpillar can then munch through the entire brood before starting its transformation into a butterfly.

DATA FILE

 DANGER FACTOR
❗ ● ● ● ●

 SIZE: Caterpillars up to 1.2 in (30 mm) long

 RANGE: Forests of Southeast Asia and Australia

DIET: Caterpillars eat ant larvae

Adult moth butterfly, top view

TASSELLED
WOBBEGONG
Eucrossorhinus dasypogon

Beneath a perfectly camouflaged skin—complete with tassels that look like seaweed fronds—there lurks a wide-jawed shark with rows of fanglike teeth. The tasselled wobbegong has the patience of an expert ambusher—anything that wanders close to the tassels is grabbed in the blink of an eye.

DATA FILE

 DANGER FACTOR
❗ ❗ ❗ ⬤ ⬤

SIZE: Up to 49.2 in (125 cm) long

RANGE: Coral reefs of New Guinea and Australia

DIET: Bottom-living fish and invertebrates

Deceivers and tricksters

HUMPBACK
ANGLERFISH
Melanocetus johnsonii

The mouth of this deep-sea fish is big enough to swallow prey that is longer than its own body. But in the darkness of the deep, it is difficult to find a meal, so the humpback anglerfish uses a "fishing line"—a glowing light on the end of a long thread which draws its victims into its jaws.

This is the larger female—males and females have smooth skin without scales.

Short-lived **males** are a **quarter** of the **size** of **females** and **lack** a **fishing line**.

A capsule containing light-producing bacteria produces the anglerfish's glow.

DATA FILE

DANGER FACTOR

SIZE: Females up to 7.1 in (18 cm) long; males up to 1.1 in (2.9 cm) long

RANGE: Deep water of open ocean worldwide

DIET: Deep-sea fish and invertebrates

Deceivers and tricksters

PIRATE PERCH
Aphredoderus sayanus

DATA FILE

 DANGER FACTOR
❗ ❗ ⚫ ⚫ ⚫

 SIZE: Up to 5.5 in (14 cm) long

 RANGE: Swamps of southeastern US

DIET: Aquatic insects, other invertebrates, and small fish

This freshwater fish hunts at night, using the sensors on its head to detect moving prey. Many small animals can avoid getting too close to other predatory fish by smelling their presence. But the pirate perch has a way of disguising its scent, so it can remain hidden—the ultimate camouflage technique.

Its **chemical camouflage** works on all its prey—**from beetles to frogs**.

A dull body helps the pirate perch hide, even by day.

Deceivers and tricksters

SOUTH AMERICAN
LEAF FISH
Monocirrhus polyacanthus

Floating head down in a rainforest creek, this stealthy hunter looks just like a drifting dead leaf. But if any other fish swims too close, the leaf fish can grab it in a fraction of a second—opening huge jaws that can swallow prey up to a third of its body length.

DATA FILE

DANGER FACTOR
! ! !

SIZE: Up to 3.1 in (8 cm) long

RANGE: Creeks and rivers of the Amazon basin

DIET: Other fish and invertebrates

Deceivers and tricksters

FALSE CLEANERFISH

Aspidontus taeniatus

There is a type of fish, called a cleaner wrasse, which plucks parasites from other fish on the reef, helping to keep them clean. The false cleanerfish looks similar to these cleaner wrasse but is really an imposter. It fools its "clients" by letting them get close for cleaning, then nips at their fins and scales.

False cleanerfish, side view

DATA FILE

 DANGER FACTOR

 SIZE: Up to 4.7 in (12 cm) long

 RANGE: Reefs of Western Pacific, including Japan and Australia

 DIET: Fins and scales of other fish, and invertebrates

Deceivers and tricksters

INDIAN OCEAN
CROCODILE FISH
Papilloculiceps longiceps

With its long crocodilelike shape and mottled brown color pattern, this big-mouthed fish has excellent camouflage. An ambush predator, it settles on the sandy or gravelly bottom of the sea, waiting motionless until another fish comes close enough to bite.

Crocodile fish, front view

DATA FILE

DANGER FACTOR

SIZE: Up to 27.5 in (70 cm) long

RANGE: Red Sea and western Indian Ocean near coasts

DIET: Other fish

Deceivers and tricksters

ALLIGATOR SNAPPING
TURTLE
Macrochelys temminckii

A lumbering meat-eating turtle needs a handy way to catch its prey. Lying underwater with its mouth wide open, the alligator snapping turtle is perfectly camouflaged with its algae-covered shell. A pink, wormlike lure in its mouth attracts passing fish, which it then bites into with a force that can snap through a broom handle.

DATA FILE

 DANGER FACTOR

 SIZE: Shell up to 31.5 in (80 cm) long

 RANGE: Freshwater swamps of southeastern US

 DIET: Fish, frogs, snakes, water birds, crayfish, and worms

Deceivers and tricksters

SIDEWINDER
Crotalus cerastes

DATA FILE

 DANGER FACTOR

 SIZE: Up to 32.3 in (82 cm) long

 RANGE: Deserts of southern US and northern Mexico

 DIET: Rodents, lizards, and insects

The sidewinder shakes the hollow scales on its tail to produce a rattling sound that warns bigger predators to stay away.

This fast-moving rattlesnake gets its name from the way it winds over desert sands in S-shaped movements—moving sideways, it throws loops of its body forward. Young sidewinders wiggle the tips of their tail to attract small lizards. As they grow older, the snakes also eat small mammals.

CANTIL
Agkistrodon bilineatus

Found in tropical dry forests and savannas, this viper either hunts or sits in ambush. The youngsters use a clever trick to bring prey within striking range—they raise their light-colored tail, which is bent at the tip, and wiggle it like a worm or a caterpillar. This maneuver easily grabs the attention of a potential victim. When the prey comes close to investigate, the cantil strikes with a deadly venomous bite.

The yellow tail tip shows up above the brown, camouflaged body.

DATA FILE

DANGER FACTOR

SIZE: Up to 54 in (138 cm) long

RANGE: Central America

DIET: Rodents, lizards, snakes, frogs, and insects

Deceivers and tricksters

PUFF ADDER

Bitis arietans

Many animals use camouflage to help them catch their prey or avoid capture. But this fearsome viper goes one step further. The puff adder disguises its scent, so it is not detected even by animals with a strong sense of smell. It is found in grasslands, deserts, and forests.

DATA FILE

DANGER FACTOR
❗ ❗ ❗ ❗ ⬤

SIZE: Up to 76 in (191 cm) long

RANGE: Africa, south of the Sahara desert

DIET: Small mammals, birds, lizards, and frogs

Deceivers and tricksters

TENTACLED SNAKE
Erpeton tentaculatum

DANGER FACTOR

SIZE: Up to 35.4 in (90 cm) long

RANGE: Swamps of Thailand, Cambodia, and Vietnam

DIET: Mainly fish

The only snake to have tentacles on its head is an underwater fisher. By anchoring its tail at the bottom of swamps, it hangs motionless in the water and waits for a fish to come close. The tentacled snake then moves its body to scare the fish into darting toward its jaws.

By anticipating the direction a fish will swim in, the snake easily catches it.

BLACK HERON

Egretta ardesiaca

DATA FILE

 DANGER FACTOR

 SIZE: 16.9–25.9 in (43–66 cm) long

 RANGE: Marshes and lakesides of Africa and Madagascar

 DIET: Fish and aquatic invertebrates

Vulnerable little fish usually swim into the shade when danger is around—and this fish-eating bird knows that. The black heron stirs the water with its feet, then arches its wings into a canopy. As startled fish swim into the cover, the bird grabs them with its long bill.

The heron makes an umbrella shape with its wings.

Black heron, side view

GREEN-BACKED
HERON
Butorides striata

You need to be quick to catch a fish, but it helps if it swims close by. The green-backed heron attracts prey with bait—by placing insects or even stolen pieces of bread in the water. It then waits for the prey to bite before lunging with its daggerlike bill.

Green-backed heron, side view

DATA FILE

DANGER FACTOR
❗ ❗ ❗ ⬤ ⬤

SIZE: 13.7–18.8 in (35–48 cm) long

RANGE: Wetlands of tropics and subtropics worldwide

DIET: Fish, amphibians, and other aquatic animals

POLAR BEAR
Ursus maritimus

DATA FILE

DANGER FACTOR

SIZE: 6.2–9.8 ft (1.9–3 m) long, head to tail

RANGE: Ice and tundra of the Arctic

DIET: Mainly seals; also other animals and carrion

The world's biggest land predator, the polar bear can weigh up to 1,543 lb (700 kg). While vulnerable seal pups are easy pickings for this carnivorous bear, it also likes to target the adult seals. The polar bear likes to ambush swimming seals at holes in the ice. When the seals come up for air in the holes, it strikes!

Hairs on the polar bear's coat are translucent rather than white—and many hairs are hollow to help trap warm air for insulation.

Deceivers and tricksters

SNOW LEOPARD
Panthera uncia

A life in the bleak mountains of Asia could be difficult for a meat-eater, but the snow leopard is superbly adapted. A champion long-jumper, it can scale rocky ridges with ease. Its pale spotted coat blends in perfectly with the stony or snow-covered land, helping it to get close enough to ambush its prey.

DATA FILE

 DANGER FACTOR

 SIZE: Up to 90.5 in (230 cm) long, head to tail

 RANGE: Central Asia, including the Himalayas

 DIET: Sheep, goats, gazelles, and rabbits

Unusually for big cats, snow leopards **cannot roar**, but **can growl** and **hiss**.

MARGAY
Leopardus wiedii

This small rainforest cat uses a sly trick to attract prey—it mimics the cries of baby monkeys, so adult monkeys come close enough to ambush. The margay's ability to grip branches firmly with both its front and back feet also helps it hunt in trees.

DATA FILE

DANGER FACTOR
❗ ❗ ❗ ◯ ◯

SIZE: 28.7–51.6 in (73–131 cm) long

RANGE: Forests of Central and South America

DIET: Rodents, opossums, and birds

ORCA
Orcinus orca

Bigger and faster than a great white shark, the orca is at the top of the ocean food chain. Also known as a killer whale, it uses lots of clever tricks to catch its prey. Orcas work together in groups to trap fish and dolphins in closed bays, and they also knock seals from floating ice floes to feed on them. They even lunge onto beaches to catch and devour their seal prey.

Orca, front view

DATA FILE

DANGER FACTOR

SIZE: 25.2–32.2 ft (7.7–9.8 m) long

RANGE: Oceans worldwide

DIET: Fish, squid, marine mammals, and seabirds

Deceivers and tricksters

123

6 DEADLY NUMBERS

Thousands of biting, stinging army ants are far more powerful than a small insect acting alone. Other animals also rely on strength in numbers to defend themselves or to catch prey.

BLUE SHARK

Prionace glauca

Many sharks prefer to hunt alone, but the blue shark—the so-called "wolf of the sea"—is often seen in packs when attacking large shoals of fish. Naturally inquisitive, it circles around a human diver many times before coming in to bite.

Blue sharks have the ability to **sense** the **heartbeats** of other fish from **miles away**.

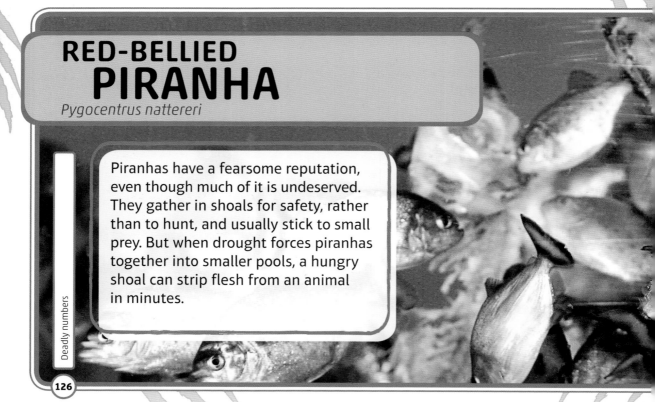

RED-BELLIED PIRANHA

Pygocentrus nattereri

Piranhas have a fearsome reputation, even though much of it is undeserved. They gather in shoals for safety, rather than to hunt, and usually stick to small prey. But when drought forces piranhas together into smaller pools, a hungry shoal can strip flesh from an animal in minutes.

Deadly numbers

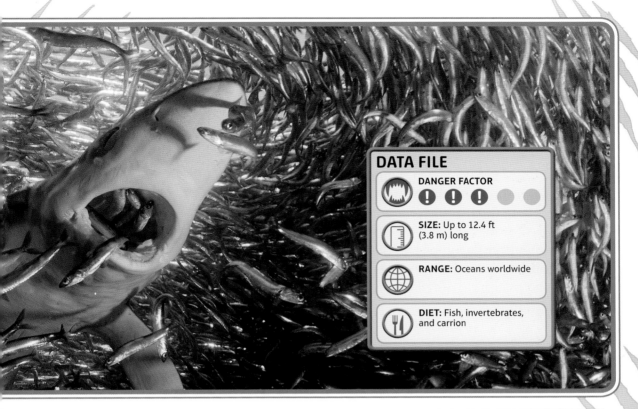

DATA FILE

DANGER FACTOR

SIZE: Up to 12.4 ft (3.8 m) long

RANGE: Oceans worldwide

DIET: Fish, invertebrates, and carrion

DATA FILE

DANGER FACTOR

SIZE: Up to 19.6 in (50 cm) long

RANGE: Creeks and ponds of the Amazon basin

DIET: Invertebrates, fish, and carrion

Red-bellied piranha, side view

GIANT MORAY EEL
Gymnothorax javanicus

Sometimes the best way to hunt is to cooperate with others. The giant moray eel partners with another predatory fish called a coral grouper. While groupers prey on other fish in open water, eels can slither between coral. Together they help to drive prey into each other's jaws, sharing the catch.

DATA FILE

DANGER FACTOR

SIZE: Up to 9.8 ft (3 m) long

RANGE: Reefs of the Indian Ocean and western Pacific

DIET: Fish and crustaceans

Deadly numbers

YELLOW-SADDLE
GOATFISH
Parupeneus cyclostomus

This brightly colored reef fish has two hunting strategies. Single goatfish can work on their own to find slow-moving prey on the sea bed. But group tactics are employed to catch faster animals that dart around the coral—attackers start the chase, while the other goatfish block off possible escape routes.

DATA FILE

DANGER FACTOR

SIZE: Up to 19.6 in (50 cm) long

RANGE: Reefs of the Red Sea, Indian Ocean, and western Pacific

DIET: Fish and invertebrates

Deadly numbers

SOCIAL
SPIDER
Stegodyphus sarasinorum

Most spiders keep strictly to themselves, but this species prefers the company of others of its kind. Hundreds of social spiders live together to build their web— and lots of them will also descend on a trapped insect. These little predators even share the meal with those who did not help in making the kill.

By working together, social spiders can easily overpower trapped prey that is a lot bigger than any single spider.

DATA FILE

 DANGER FACTOR
❗ ❗ ⚪ ⚪ ⚪

 SIZE: 0.2–0.4 in (6–12 mm) long, head and body

 RANGE: Dry woodlands of southern Asia

DIET: Insects

WESTERN
HONEYBEE
Apis mellifera

A colony of honeybees contains thousands of workers laboring together to feed their hive. Even though each is armed with a painful defensive stinger, honeybees are not usually aggressive around humans. But in parts of America, aggressive species resulting from crosses with African bees are more likely to attack in big swarms.

DATA FILE

 DANGER FACTOR
❗ ❗ ○ ○ ○

 SIZE: Workers 0.3–0.5 in (10–15 mm) long

 RANGE: Almost worldwide, except near the cold poles

 DIET: Nectar and pollen

Deadly numbers

131

ASIAN GIANT HORNET
Vespa mandarinia

The stinger of this fearsome predator is four times bigger than that of a honeybee. The bee uses its stinger for defense, but for this hornet, it is also a weapon of attack. Asian giant hornets raid hives to kill anything alive, biting off the bees' heads and dragging victims away to feed their young.

DATA FILE

 DANGER FACTOR

SIZE: 1.5–1.8 in (38–45 mm) long

RANGE: Forests in Japan, China, and Southeast Asia

DIET: Bees, beetles, caterpillars, and other social insects

AFRICAN DRIVER ANT

Dorylus

Sharp pincerlike jaws are powered by muscles inside the ant's huge head.

A marching column of up to 50 million driver ants in search of prey is a formidable foe. Each line is flanked by big-headed soldiers that bite their victims and don't let go. These ants have such strong jaws that local people use them to clamp together open wounds.

DATA FILE

DANGER FACTOR

❗❗❗ ◯ ◯

SIZE: Worker ants 0.07–0.6 in (2–15 mm) long; biggest are called soldiers

RANGE: Grasslands and woodlands of Africa and southern Asia

DIET: Ground-living invertebrates, such as earthworms and insects

Deadly numbers

TROPICAL AMERICAN
ARMY ANT
Eciton burchellii

A swarm of 200,000 ants is already intimidating, but it is even scarier if they are meat-eating army ants. These ferocious creatures have stingers and enormous jaws that can pierce human flesh. Virtually blind, they stick together using chemical signals to communicate as they sweep over the rainforest floor, tearing to pieces anything that comes in their way.

Deadly numbers

DATA FILE

DANGER FACTOR

! ! ! ● ●

SIZE: Workers 0.1–0.5 in (3–12 mm) long

RANGE: Rainforests of Central and South America

DIET: Insects and other small animals

FOSSA
Cryptoprocta ferox

The top predator on the island of Madagascar is the fossa, an agile climber that often hunts in groups. As one fossa chases a lemur to the ground, another will wait below to grab it. A catlike animal, it is active during both day and night.

DATA FILE

DANGER FACTOR
❗ ❗ ❗ ⚪ ⚪

SIZE: 53–59 in (135–150 cm) long, from head to tail

RANGE: Forests of Madagascar

DIET: Mainly lemurs, birds, snakes, lizards, and turtles

Deadly numbers

HARRIS'S
HAWK

Parabuteo unicinctus

Food can be difficult to find in a desert, but Harris's hawk uses a trick that sets it apart from other birds of prey—it cooperates with others. Small groups of these birds work together when they hunt, helping each other to scan the landscape, with one or two flushing the prey out from the depths of its cover.

Large feet with long talons help this hawk bring down much larger prey than other birds of prey of the same size.

DATA FILE

DANGER FACTOR
❗ ❗ ❗ ○ ○

SIZE: 19–22 in (48–56 cm) long

RANGE: Desert and savanna of Central and South America

DIET: Mammals up to the size of rabbits; also birds and lizards

Members of a **group share** the **meat** after making a **kill**.

SOUTH AMERICAN
COATI
Nasua nasua

South American coati, front view

Coatis are long-nosed relatives of raccoons that roam the rainforest floor in bands of up to 65, grabbing small animals disturbed by their antics. Anything with stingers, fangs, or spines—such as scorpions or tarantulas—are rolled around until they are dead or disarmed. Predatory birds learn to follow coatis to catch anything that's trying to get away.

DATA FILE

 DANGER FACTOR

 SIZE: 33.4–44.4 in (85–113 cm) long, head to tail

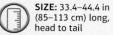 **RANGE:** Forests of northern South America

 DIET: Invertebrates, rodents, fish, crabs, and fruits

SPOTTED HYENA
Crocuta crocuta

30 hyenas can **strip flesh off** a large **antelope** in just **13** minutes.

A short snout helps give the hyena a stronger, bone-cracking bite.

Hyenas are often thought of as scavengers, picking up leftovers from other kills. But the spotted hyena usually kills to eat—getting up to 95 percent of food by hunting. Packs of hyenas do not rely on stalking prey—they can chase an antelope at speed over several miles. When the prey is exhausted, the pack descends and kills by tearing it to pieces.

DATA FILE

 DANGER FACTOR

 SIZE: 57.8–73.6 in (147–187 cm) long, head to tail

 RANGE: Grasslands and open woodlands of Africa

 DIET: Hoofed mammals and other prey; also carrion

Deadly numbers

GRAY WOLF

Canis lupus

DATA FILE

DANGER FACTOR
! ! ! !

SIZE: 48–71.6 in (122–182 cm) long

RANGE: Forests and open country of the Northern Hemisphere

DIET: Deer, pigs, birds, and carrion

In the depths of winter, when food can be limited, wolves come together to hunt in packs. Together they can chase a deer for up to 3.1 miles (5 km) before it falls from exhaustion. Pack hunting means that meat must be shared, and it is less likely that there will be any left for roaming scavengers.

Gray wolf, side view

Deadly numbers

AFRICAN WILD
DOG
Lycaon pictus

DANGER FACTOR

SIZE: 45.6–72 in
(116–183 cm) long

RANGE: Grasslands and
open woodlands of Africa

DIET: Mainly antelopes and
gazelles; also hares, lizards,
and bird eggs

Running at speeds of up to 37 mph
(60 km/h) under the African sun, a pack of
African wild dogs work as a team to bring
down larger prey. When one dog reaches
the victim, it bites its nose and holds on
to wait for the other members of the
pack to make the final kill.

Strong canines can stab
through thick hide.

African wild dog, side view

Deadly numbers

LION
Panthera leo

Africa's top predators, lions—the so-called social cats—are the only cats known to work as a team. By working as a team, a pride of lions can increase the chance of making a kill by more than 10 percent. They stalk their prey to get close enough for an ambush, then give chase—with some of the pride running ahead to cut off their prey's escape route.

Female lions—without a mane—do most of the hunting.

Hoofed mammals, such as this greater kudu (a kind of antelope), are a lion's favorite prey.

Up to **20 percent** of lion **kills** are **lost** to **spotted hyenas**.

DATA FILE

DANGER FACTOR
! ! ! ! !

SIZE: 7.2–11.4 ft (2.2–3.5 m) long, head to tail

RANGE: Open landscapes of Africa and northwestern India

DIET: Animals up to the size of giraffes; also carrion

7 SKILLS, TACTICS, AND CUNNING

Super senses, athletic skills, and brain power are the ultimate tools of survival—and in the struggle of life, they help clever predators stay one step ahead of their prey.

HUMBOLDT SQUID
Dosidicus gigas

This ocean predator is popularly known as the "Red Devil," as it flashes red when it becomes aggressive. The Humboldt squid gathers in packs of more than a thousand, possibly to help trap prey. However, if they bunch too close, they turn on each other—and aggressive squid may even attack human divers.

Like other kinds of squid, this animal has fins to help stabilize its swimming in the water.

BOLAS SPIDER
Mastophorinae

This nocturnal spider has a special trick to catch moths—its preferred prey. The wings of moths are covered in tiny scales, which help them slip from a web when they are caught. This spider solves this problem by not spinning a web like a net. Instead it swings around a sticky thread with its legs to catch any moth that flies close.

DATA FILE

 DANGER FACTOR

 SIZE: 0.07–0.5 in (2–15 mm) long, head and body

 RANGE: Forests of America, Africa, Asia, and Australia

 DIET: Moths

Skills, tactics, and cunning

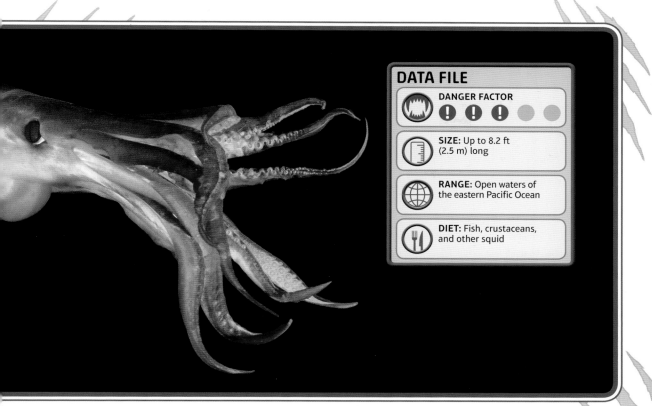

The bolas spider produces a **scent** that **attracts moths** so they come close enough to catch.

Each droplet is a special kind of silk that works like glue to stick to a flying moth.

Skills, tactics, and cunning

RED-VEINED
DARTER
Sympetrum fonscolombii

Not many insects can beat a dragonfly when it comes to hunting while in flight. Its massive compound eyes—which cover most of the head—can sense the darting movements of tiny flies. The dragonfly waits on a leaf before darting into the air to snatch its target with gripping legs. It then returns to its perch to feed.

The dragonfly arranges its hairy legs into a basket so it can scoop up prey while in flight.

The red-veined darter has a black-edged golden patch on the tip of its wing.

Each **compound eye** contains thousands of **tiny lenses**.

DATA FILE

DANGER FACTOR
❗ ❗ ⚪ ⚪ ⚪

SIZE: 1.2–1.5 in (32–40 mm) long

RANGE: Swamps of Europe, Africa, and Asia

DIET: Other smaller insects

Skills, tactics, and cunning

ELECTRIC
EEL
Electrophorus electricus

This fish uses shock tactics for hunting and self-defense. It has lines of tiny batterylike organs running through its long body. When these work together, they can fire a bolt of electricity up to 500 volts. This shockwave can kill smaller animals and is enough to stun a full-grown human.

DANGER FACTOR

SIZE: Up to 98.4 in (250 cm) long

RANGE: Swamps of the Amazon basin

DIET: Other fish, small mammals, and invertebrates

Electric eel, side view

TEXAS HORNED LIZARD
Phrynosoma cornutum

Having a hard, spiky body helps this little lizard deter predators. It also has a surprising trick to keep its enemies away—it can squirt toxic blood. When faced with danger, the lizard squeezes a blood vessel in the corners of its eyes and shoots blood into the face of its attacker. A foul-tasting chemical in the blood repulses the predator, driving it away.

DATA FILE

 DANGER FACTOR
❗ ● ● ● ●

 SIZE: Up to 2.7 in (7 cm) long

 RANGE: Deserts of southern US

 DIET: Mainly ants; sometimes other insects

Skills, tactics, and cunning

COMMON LANCEHEAD

Bothrops atrox

This forest-living pit viper can track down its prey even in the darkness of night. The heat-sensitive pits in front of its eyes help it pick up the body warmth of small animals, such as mice and rats. Once detected, the victim is attacked with a venomous bite that kills within minutes.

DATA FILE

 DANGER FACTOR

 SIZE: Up to 98.4 in (250 cm) long

 RANGE: Central America and northwestern South America

 DIET: Small mammals, birds, lizards, and other snakes

Skills, tactics, and cunning

SPITTING COBRA
Naja mossambica

DATA FILE

 DANGER FACTOR
! ! ! ! ○

 SIZE: Up to 60.6 in (154 cm) long

 RANGE: Savanna of southeastern Africa

 DIET: Rodents, birds, frogs, and other snakes

No other snake defends itself quite like a spitting cobra. It has a venomous bite, but its fangs have tiny forward-facing holes, so they also spray venom through the air. This venom does not kill the victim—but the cobra aims for the eyes, and a direct hit can cause permanent blindness.

This snake can **spit** its **venom** at a target up to **10 ft (3 m)** away.

By rearing up and pulling its head back, the cobra can spit farther ahead.

Skills, tactics, and cunning

BROWN
SKUA
Catharacta antarctica

Skuas regularly **steal eggs** and **chicks** from **penguin colonies**.

Skuas are the pirates of the bird world. They attack gulls and other birds to make them drop their food—sometimes even making them throw up their last meal. But these pirates are murderous, too—they kill birds by dragging them out to sea and drowning them.

Skills, tactics, and cunning

DATA FILE

DANGER FACTOR
! ! !

SIZE: 20.4–25.1 in (52–64 cm) long

RANGE: Islands and coastlines of the Southern Ocean

DIET: Other seabirds, plus chicks and eggs; also carrion

BARN OWL
Tyto alba

Few other nighttime predators can match the skill of a barn owl. As it waits on a branch or hovers over the ground, its super-sensitive hearing can track a moving mouse in complete darkness. Once caught, prey is carried back in its bill to a perch, ready to be eaten.

DATA FILE

 DANGER FACTOR
❗❗❗

 SIZE: 11.4–17.3 in (29–44 cm) long

 RANGE: Worldwide, except far north North America and most of Asia

 DIET: Mainly small mammals; sometimes other animals

The barn owl's face has a flat, **heart-shaped disk** to help **intensify** faint **sounds** from prey.

Skills, tactics, and cunning

GOLDEN EAGLE

Aquila chrysaetos

This eagle's wingspan can be up to 7.5 ft (2.3 m) long.

A big golden eagle can weigh more than 13 lb (6 kg) and has the power to kill prey up to the size of a full-grown swan. It can even tackle other predators, such as foxes and cats. The eagle strikes its target by coming in low and knocking its prey down with the strength of a blow before killing it with its huge talons.

DATA FILE

DANGER FACTOR

SIZE: 29.5–35.4 in
(75–90 cm) long

RANGE: Open country of
the Northern Hemisphere

DIET: Mainly mammals,
birds, and carrion

A golden eagle's
deadly talons are over
2.7 in (7 cm) long.

Golden eagles
**smash tortoise
shells** by **dropping
them on rocks.**

PEREGRINE
FALCON
Falco peregrinus

A peregrine falcon scans for prey—such as a flapping pigeon—from a topmost perch or from soaring high in the sky. It then gives chase, culminating with a dive-bombing stoop that breaks all animal speed records, before the target is caught and killed midair.

A peregrine falcon can **reach** more than **199 mph (320 km/h)** in a **midair dive**.

DATA FILE

DANGER FACTOR

SIZE: 13.3–19.6 in (34–50 cm) long

RANGE: Various habitats on every continent except Antarctica

DIET: Mainly other birds; sometimes mammals, insects, and reptiles

GREAT GREY
SHRIKE
Lanius excubitor

Shrikes can kill animals up to **four times** their **own body size**.

The shrike's bill is strong enough to break its prey's neck.

Impaled prey is used as a pantry or to mark the shrike's territory.

This bird is only slightly bigger than a starling, but it has bloodthirsty habits. It perches on its lookout—a branch or a wire—to watch for movement. The shrike then dives to the ground to kill the prey with its hooked beak. It sometimes impales the bodies on thorns for eating later.

DATA FILE

DANGER FACTOR
❗❗

SIZE: 9.4–9.8 in (24–25 cm) long

RANGE: Open country across the Northern Hemisphere

DIET: Insects; other birds; and small animals, such as voles

Skills, tactics, and cunning

GHOST **BAT**
Macroderma gigas

This Australian bat is sometimes called a false vampire, but it's not a sneaky blood-sucker. Instead, the ghost bat is a meat-eating killer. It swoops down from a tree onto a target, such as a mouse, and folds its wings around the struggling animal to deliver a deadly bite to the head or neck.

DATA FILE

DANGER FACTOR

SIZE: 3.9–5.5 in (10–14 cm) long; wingspan up to 23.6 in (60 cm)

RANGE: Forest and grasslands with caves in northern Australia

DIET: Small mammals, birds, reptiles, and invertebrates

Skills, tactics, and cunning

STOAT
Mustela erminea

Despite weighing less than a guinea pig, the stoat is a fearless hunter and can kill an animal up to the size of a full-grown hare. This speedy little predator listens and smells for prey, hunting in a zigzag pattern—sometimes chasing its victim right into their home burrow.

The stoat **kills** its prey with a **bite** to the **base** of the **victim's skull**.

Skills, tactics, and cunning

CHEETAH
Acinonyx jubatus

By inching, unseen, closer to its target, a cheetah makes sure a chase to the kill is short. It cannot keep its top speed for more than a minute, but during that time hits 62 mph (100 km/h)—the fastest sprint of any animal. When it has caught up with its prey, this agile hunter knocks the victim off balance with a slap of its paw.

DATA FILE

DANGER FACTOR

SIZE: 5.9–7.2 ft (1.8–2.2 m) long, head to tail

RANGE: Grasslands and open woodlands in Africa

DIET: Mainly small antelopes, such as gazelles

Skills, tactics, and cunning

BOTTLENOSE DOLPHIN

Tursiops

DATA FILE

DANGER FACTOR

SIZE: 6.2–12.4 ft (1.9–3.8 m) long

RANGE: Oceans worldwide, except for the coldest waters around the poles

DIET: Fish, squid, and octopuses

Seeing prey can be a problem in gloomy or murky waters. In such conditions, dolphins use a technique called echolocation—they make clicking sounds which bounce back from objects, including fish, as an echo. By listening for the echo, dolphins can work out the position of their next meal.

Skills, tactics, and cunning

CHIMPANZEE
Pan troglodytes

The chimpanzee is the most carnivorous of the great apes and is a smart hunter, using many tactics to get food. Some chimps use plant stems to "fish" for insects in termite mounds. Others are more bloodthirsty and skewer bushbabies (a type of small primate) with sharp sticks. Chimpanzees also work as a team to chase and catch monkeys in trees.

Skills, tactics, and cunning

Male chimpanzees are **in charge** when **groups hunt** down monkeys.

DATA FILE

DANGER FACTOR
! ! ! !

SIZE: 27.5–37.7 in (70–96 cm) long

RANGE: Forests of western and central Africa

DIET: Fruits, vegetation, eggs, and animals

Skills, tactics, and cunning

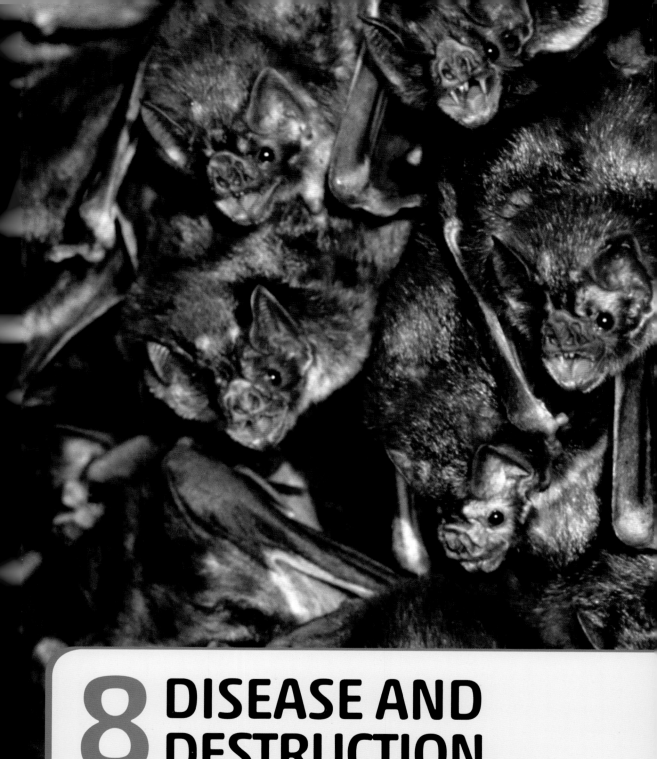

8 DISEASE AND DESTRUCTION

Sometimes the most dangerous animals of all are not necessarily the flesh-eating carnivores. Blood-sucking animals, such as vampire bats, inflict irritating bites, but it is the disease they carry that can kill many.

ROSY WOLFSNAIL
Euglandina rosea

Snails can be easy prey, especially for the carnivorous wolfsnail. To catch its food, the wolfsnail just follows its prey's slime trail. Smaller snails are swallowed whole, while bigger ones are eaten inside their shell. This species was introduced to the Pacific Islands in the hope that it would eat giant snail pests—but it ended up driving many smaller species to extinction.

DATA FILE

 DANGER FACTOR

 SIZE: Shell up to 3.1 in (8 cm) long

 RANGE: North and Central America; introduced elsewhere

 DIET: Other snails

CHINESE MITTEN CRAB
Eriocheir sinensis

Named for the mittenlike mat of hair on its pincers, this Asian crab has hitchhiked around the world on ships, finding its way to Europe and North America. It causes damage by burrowing into river banks, and its aggressive behavior can harm other animals. This crab also poses a threat to human health, as it is a host to various parasites.

DATA FILE

 DANGER FACTOR

 SIZE: Body up to 3.9 in (10 cm) wide

 RANGE: Estuaries of eastern Asia; introduced elsewhere

 DIET: Wide range of invertebrates, fish, and carrion

Disease and destruction

169

ANOPHELES
MOSQUITO
Anopheles

Anopheles mosquito, side view

A small buzzing insect doesn't look like a killer. But 15 percent of anopheles species carry malaria—a disease that kills over a million people every year. Males drink harmlessly from nectar, but females need blood to make their eggs. When they pierce the skin to reach it, they inject the victim with the deadly malaria parasites.

DATA FILE

DANGER FACTOR

SIZE: Wingspan 0.2–0.3 in (5.5–7 mm), depending on species

RANGE: Almost worldwide; malaria-carriers are tropical

DIET: Females suck blood of animals

AUSTRALIAN PARALYSIS TICK

Ixodes holocyclus

Ticks are relatives of spiders. They feed by sucking the blood of animals. Like some other ticks, this Australian species can carry dangerous bacteria in its bite. Its saliva also contains a poison that paralyzes muscles and can ultimately stop the heart.

DATA FILE

DANGER FACTOR

SIZE: 0.2 in (3–4 mm) long, when unfed

RANGE: Eastern coast of Australia

DIET: Blood of kangaroos, koalas, and humans

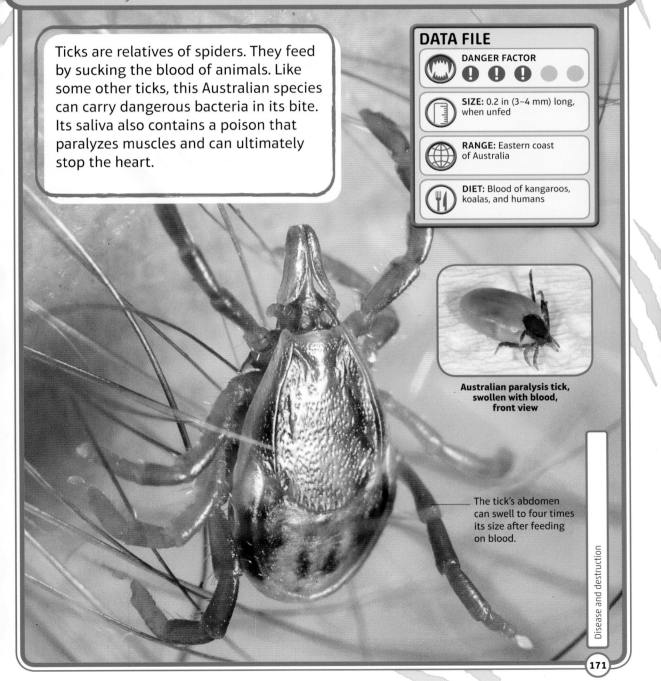

Australian paralysis tick, swollen with blood, front view

The tick's abdomen can swell to four times its size after feeding on blood.

TSETSE FLY

Glossina

DATA FILE

DANGER FACTOR

SIZE: 0.2–0.6 in
(6–16 mm) long

RANGE: Grasslands and
open woodlands in Africa

DIET: Blood of vertebrates,
including humans

Tsetse flies are totally dependent on blood as their food. Their bite is painful and can also be dangerous. Six species of these blood suckers carry parasites that enter the body during a bite and cause a disease, called sleeping sickness, that kills about 10,000 humans every year.

The skin of this fly's abdomen is stretchy, so its body can swell with blood as the fly feeds.

Disease and destruction

ORIENTAL RAT
FLEA
Xenopsylla cheopis

DATA FILE

 DANGER FACTOR

 SIZE: 0.05–0.1 in (1.5–4 mm) long

 RANGE: Worldwide in the nests of black rats

 DIET: Blood of rats and other mammals, including humans

Fleas are flightless, jumping insects that feed by biting animals to suck their blood. This infamous species lives on black rats but can spread plague-causing bacteria to humans. The plague is a deadly disease that killed up to 50 million people during the Black Death of the 1300s, and still occurs in parts of the world today.

Disease and destruction

ELECTRIC ANT

Wasmannia auropunctata

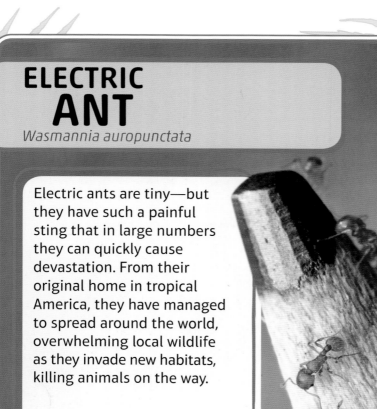

On the **Galápagos Islands**, electric ants **eat baby tortoises**.

Electric ants are tiny—but they have such a painful sting that in large numbers they can quickly cause devastation. From their original home in tropical America, they have managed to spread around the world, overwhelming local wildlife as they invade new habitats, killing animals on the way.

DATA FILE

DANGER FACTOR

SIZE: Workers 0.03–0.07 in (1–2 mm) long

RANGE: Various habitats in tropical America; introduced elsewhere

DIET: Animals, seeds, plants, and honeydew

CROWN-OF-THORNS STARFISH

Acanthaster planci

Many kinds of animals feed on coral but, with its venomous spines, this giant coral-eating starfish is protected from bigger predators. On Australia's Great Barrier Reef, huge numbers of these starfish appear every few years—and they munch their way through so much coral that it cannot easily grow back.

DATA FILE

 DANGER FACTOR

 SIZE: More than 27.5 in (70 cm) in diameter

 RANGE: Coral reefs of Indian and Pacific Oceans

DIET: Coral

SNAKEHEAD

Channa

Snakehead, side view

The large mouth of an adult snakehead is big enough to swallow birds or small mammals.

Snakeheads grow to be big predatory fish that can breathe air and, remarkably, can survive long enough on land to wiggle from one pond to another. In parts of North America, snakeheads kept as pets or for food have been released and now threaten to invade wetland habitats.

DATA FILE

 DANGER FACTOR

 SIZE: Up to 3.9 ft (1.2 m) long, depending on species

 RANGE: Swamps of (tropical) Africa and Asia; introduced elsewhere

 DIET: Mainly fish, frogs, and invertebrates

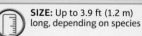

NILE PERCH

Lates niloticus

DANGER FACTOR

SIZE: Up to 6.5 ft (2 m) long

RANGE: Rivers, lakes, and canals of Africa

DIET: Fish and invertebrates

The natural home of this large fish is in African rivers, such as the Nile and the Congo. But in the 1950s, it was introduced to lakes in eastern Africa as food for humans. These lakes contained hundreds of fish species found nowhere else, but the Nile perch became the new top predator and drove many species to extinction.

The Nile perch **wiped out** over **200** fish species from Africa's **Lake Victoria**.

Disease and destruction

RED LIONFISH
Pterois volitans

The magnificent fins of a lionfish carry venomous spines that deliver a painful defensive sting. The fins also spread outward to scare and drive prey into a corner. Its natural home is the Pacific Ocean, but introduced lionfish have invaded the Atlantic, where their big appetite for defenseless sea animals has damaged populations of native wildlife species.

DATA FILE

DANGER FACTOR

SIZE: Up to 14.9 in (38 cm) long

RANGE: Coastal waters of the western Pacific Ocean; introduced elsewhere

DIET: Other fish, shrimp, and crabs

CANE TOAD
Rhinella marina

DATA FILE

 DANGER FACTOR

 SIZE: Up to 9.8 in (25 cm) long

RANGE: Tropical America; introduced elsewhere

 DIET: Invertebrates and other small animals

In 1935, a few thousand cane toads—from tropical America—were set free in Australia in the hope that they would eat the beetle pests of sugar cane. They failed to control the beetles—instead, the toads preyed on native animals, and many natural predators died from eating the toad's poisonous skin. Today, there may be more than 1 billion cane toads spread throughout Australia.

Disease and destruction

BROWN TREE SNAKE
Boiga irregularis

In the 1950s, brown tree snakes were spotted on the Pacific island of Guam—over 2,485 miles (4,000 km) away from their home in Australia. After being accidentally introduced by a cargo ship, the reptile has multiplied to kill almost all of Guam's vulnerable birdlife—unused to dangerous predators and unable to defend themselves against an invasion of venomous snakes.

The brown tree snake holds its body in an S-shape loop to help it strike with deadly accuracy.

DATA FILE

DANGER FACTOR

SIZE: Up to 9.8 ft (3 m) long

RANGE: New Guinea and Australia; introduced to Pacific islands

DIET: Small mammals, birds, eggs, and lizards

BROWN RAT

Rattus norvegicus

Gnawing rats cause **$1 billion** of damage in the US each year.

DATA FILE

DANGER FACTOR

SIZE: Up to 15.7 in (40 cm) long, head to tail

RANGE: Originally from China, but now spread throughout the world

DIET: Wide variety of plant and animal foods

Rats followed humans around the world as stowaways on ships—and the brown rat is now found on every continent except Antarctica. They are intelligent rodents that adapt well to new surroundings and food supplies. Brown rats will eat eggs, birds, and lizards, and—on islands—have driven many defenseless species to the verge of extinction.

Disease and destruction

VAMPIRE BAT
Desmodus rotundus

At night, a vampire bat flutters down near a target—usually a sleeping chicken, cow, or human—and quietly crawls closer, like a spider. The victim rarely feels its sharp, pointed teeth bite and its tongue lapping the blood. The bite itself is not dangerous, but some bats transmit a deadly disease called rabies.

DATA FILE

 DANGER FACTOR
 SIZE: 2.7–3.5 in (7–9 cm) long; wingspan 13.7–15.7 in (35–40 cm)

 RANGE: Forests and open habitats of South America

 DIET: Blood of large mammals and birds

Disease and destruction

Vampire bat, front view

Heat sensors on the nose help the vampire bat to home in on warm-blooded prey.

Razor-sharp incisor teeth in the upper and lower jaws draw blood by slicing a circle of skin from their victim.

After **feeding**, bats may **share** their food with others by **regurgitating** it.

DOMESTIC
CAT
Felis catus

DATA FILE

DANGER FACTOR
! ! !

SIZE: 23.6–35.4 in (60–90 cm) long, head to tail

RANGE: Virtually worldwide

DIET: Small mammals, birds, and other animals

Domesticated cats probably originated from the wildcat species found in Egypt 4,000 years ago. Since then, humans have carried them around the world to control rats and mice, and as pets. Some, called feral cats, now live permanently away from humans. But all cats remain hunters and kill millions of birds and other wildlife each year.

A species of **flightless wren** in New Zealand was **wiped out** by **cats**.

Disease and destruction

RED
FOX
Vulpes vulpes

DATA FILE

DANGER FACTOR

SIZE: 28.7–54.7 in (73–139 cm) long, head to tail

RANGE: North America, Europe, and Asia; introduced elsewhere

DIET: Small animals, carrion, and human trash

People introduced red foxes to Australia in 1855, because they wanted to hunt them for sport. But within a century, these carnivores had spread through the continent to prey on marsupials, ground-nesting birds, and turtles— causing a decline in much of Australia's wildlife. Today, red foxes still threaten many of Australia's species.

Red foxes have **invaded 76 percent** of the Australian continent.

Disease and destruction

COMMON
HIPPOPOTAMUS
Hippopotamus amphibius

A 4-ton, bad-tempered animal with the biggest mouth of a creature on land is certainly formidable. Hippopotamuses can sometimes trample crops and eat so much vegetation that they cause land erosion. Despite being plant-eaters, they have massive canine teeth, which big males will sometimes use as a weapon in territorial battles. Females, protecting their calves, have overturned boats and attacked occupants in defense.

DATA FILE

DANGER FACTOR
! ! ! ! !

SIZE: 10.8–18.3 ft (3.3–5.6 m) long, head to tail

RANGE: Grasslands of Africa, near water

DIET: Mainly vegetation

A hippopotamus can open its **mouth** as wide as **150 degrees**.

The lower canines of a hippopotamus can grow up to 11.8 in (30 cm) above the gum line, and each can weigh up to 6.6 lb (3 kg).

MOOSE
Alces alces

Moose are the world's biggest type of deer—and in Alaska and Siberia, bulls (males) can weigh up to 1,697 lb (770 kg). Aggressive bulls, defending their females, thrash the vegetation with their enormous antlers and may charge humans. Large moose wandering near roads may even collide with moving cars—with fatal consequences.

DATA FILE

 DANGER FACTOR
 ! !

 SIZE: 8.2–10.4 ft (2.5–3.2 m) long, head to tail

RANGE: Marshy forests across the Northern Hemisphere

 DIET: Trees, shrubs, and aquatic plants

CAPE BUFFALO

Syncerus caffer

The span of a Cape buffalo's horns can reach more than 3 ft (1 m), making them impressive weapons. Displaying males show off their horns to one another but rarely inflict injury. Instead, their horns are deadlier when used in self-defense—charging buffalos are said to be one of the most dangerous big animals in Africa.

DATA FILE

DANGER FACTOR

SIZE: 9.5–14.7 ft (2.9–4.5 m) long, head to tail

RANGE: Grasslands of eastern and southern Africa

DIET: Grass

Disease and destruction

189

AFRICAN SAVANNA
ELEPHANT
Loxodonta africana

The African savanna elephant is the world's heaviest land animal—males can weigh up to 11 tons when fully grown. Life in an elephant herd is usually peaceful, and there are strong bonds between females. But elephants in a herd will fiercely defend the calves in their care, and male elephants become especially aggressive during the breeding season.

Elephants have **thick pads** in their feet that help **support** their **weight**.

DATA FILE

DANGER FACTOR
! ! ! !

SIZE: 22.9–29.5 ft (7–9 m) long, trunk to tail

RANGE: Grasslands and woodlands of Africa

DIET: Grass, leaves, stalks, fruits, bark, and roots

Apart from humans, no predators typically attack full-grown elephants, but lions and elephants may clash when one or the other is defending their family group.

9
REFERENCE

There are good reasons why some animals are dangerous. Over millions of years, evolution has given animals the best tools to survive. Predators must kill to feed themselves or their offspring, and all animals must defend themselves from an attack, even if sometimes it means killing their attacker.

POISONS AND VENOMS

Poisons cause harm when they are eaten, but venoms are harmful when injected through bites or with stingers. It usually takes energy to produce these dangerous substances, so animals will only use them if they have to. At first, a venomous snake may attack with a "dry bite" that lacks venom, but it comes as a warning of the real danger that might follow.

DEFENDING WITH POISON

The best poisonous defense is for an animal to produce a chemical that tastes so bad that any predator will let go as soon as it bites—and so learns not to try again. But some poisons can have lethal side effects.

Golden poison frog
Poison in this frog's skin causes unpleasant numbness, so a predator will quickly let go. But if the poison gets inside the predator's body, it paralyzes muscles and causes heart failure. It is one of the deadliest poisons known.

Monarch butterfly caterpillar
This caterpillar becomes poisonous by eating leaves of the milkweed plant. Birds and other animals that eat this caterpillar become violently sick, so they learn to avoid anything with this yellow-and-black warning pattern.

ATTACKING WITH VENOM

About 25 percent of snake species produce venom. Before becoming fatal, venoms may immobilize the victim, so it cannot injure the snake by fighting back. The rattlesnake (below) is an example of a snake that uses venom to attack its prey.

1. Sensing the prey
A rattlesnake flicks its tongue to pick up odors from prey and then locate them.

2. Deadly bite
Venom sacs release their contents from fang tips during a bite.

3. Swallowing whole
Once killed by venom, the prey is swallowed head first.

HOW STINGERS WORK

Stingers need to have a sharp harpoon to puncture skin. A sac of venom is connected to the harpoon through a system of tubing. When the harpoon strikes, venom flows along the tubing and is injected.

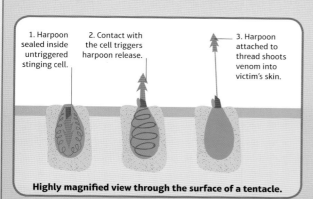

1. Harpoon sealed inside untriggered stinging cell.

2. Contact with the cell triggers harpoon release.

3. Harpoon attached to thread shoots venom into victim's skin.

Highly magnified view through the surface of a tentacle.

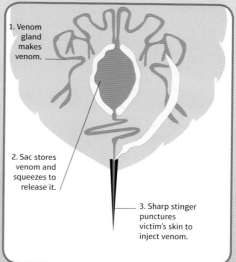

1. Venom gland makes venom.

2. Sac stores venom and squeezes to release it.

3. Sharp stinger punctures victim's skin to inject venom.

Jellyfish stinger
Tentacles of jellyfish are coated with microscopic stinging cells. When touched, their tiny harpoons automatically fire to inject their venom.

Hornet stinger
Like bees and wasps, hornets carry their stingers at the rear of their body and use them to stab through skin to inject venom.

HOW PAINFUL?

In 1983, American insect expert Justin Schmidt came up with a pain scale to compare the stings of different insects. His descriptions were based on personal experience: he deliberately let a variety of wasps, bees, and ants sting him before describing what he felt.

Sweat bee
Its sting feels like a tiny spark has singed a single hair on your arm.

Bald-faced hornet
The sting feels like getting your hand squashed in a revolving door.

STING RATING

0	1.0	2.0

Schmidt used his scale to **rank** the stings of **78 species** of stinging insects.

Southern fire ant
The effects of this mild sting last less than 5 minutes.

Bullhorn acacia ant
This sting is as painful as getting a staple fired into your hand.

Common wasp
The sting is likened
to a matchstick being
extinguished on your tongue.

Maricopa harvester ant
This sting feels like
8 hours of drilling into
an ingrown toenail.

Tarantula hawk
One of the most painful
stings, it is blinding, fierce,
and shockingly electric.

2.0   3.0   4.0

Honeybee
Its sting is as painful as
that of a common wasp.

Red paper wasp
A sting from this wasp
would be as painful as
spilling acid on a paper cut.

Bullet ant
This sting is like walking over
flaming charcoal with a 3-inch
nail lodged in your heel.

DEADLY DEFENDERS

If staying hidden under cover doesn't work, for many animals the best way to stay safe is to run, swim, or fly away from danger. But if cornered or trapped, all animals will attempt to fight back. And they may use defenses that can injure their attacker—sometimes with deadly consequences.

Warning colors and patterns

Bright colors or patterns in the animal kingdom—especially red, yellow, black, or white—are sometimes a signal warning of possible danger and are used to keep predators away. A predator learns to associate a painful sting or a nasty taste with warning colors, so it will avoid similar-looking prey in future. Some harmless species have even evolved to imitate dangerous ones, so they stay protected without having to make any poison.

Skunk
The black-and-white pattern of a defensive skunk warns predators away. When threatened, the skunk sprays a foul liquid from glands near its bottom. Although not lethal, it is smelly enough to repel predators.

Coral snake
Bands of red, yellow, and black make this rainforest snake stand out and send out a warning that its bite can deliver deadly venom.

Kingsnake
This nonvenomous snake copies the banding pattern of the deadly coral snake, fooling predators into thinking it has a dangerous bite.

Deadly in numbers

A single honeybee has limited stinging power—and may die if its stinger gets stuck in the thick skin of a creature as big as a human. But many bees swarming together can easily deter large attackers. Like many social insects, each agitated bee also releases an alarm chemical, which attracts more bees to join the attack.

Dangerous defenders

Some animals use weapons in defense. For instance, injuries caused by a porcupine's spine might occasionally prove fatal for an attacker. But the deadliest defenders are those that use poisons or venoms or rely on their bulk and physical strength to fight back.

MOST-DEADLY DEFENDER

Cape buffalo
Poor eyesight, sharp horns, and an aggressive temper can result in a deadly charge.

Hippopotamus
A giant mouth with enormous canines can deliver a devastating bite.

Poison frog
The skin of this tiny frog contains enough poison to kill 10 grown men.

Cobra
A bite from a cobra can inject fast-acting venom that paralyzes muscles.

African savanna elephant
Breeding males and mothers with calves will aggressively charge any attacker.

Musk ox
A circle of musk ox—each facing outward with sharp horns—makes for a dangerous group defense.

Bombardier beetle
This beetle fires a hot, stinging discharge of chemicals from the rear of its body.

Porcupine
A threatened porcupine charges backward and can impale even a large predator with its long, pointed spines.

Surgeonfish
Razor-sharp spines on either side of this fish's tail can slash the flesh of an attacker.

Gazelle
A gazelle uses speed to run from an attacker but will jab with its horns if cornered.

LEAST-DEADLY DEFENDER

Reference

EXTINCT KILLERS

Fossils of prehistoric creatures show that deadly weapons are nothing new. Long-extinct animals used jaws, teeth, and horns to kill or in self-defense. By studying fossils, scientists can sometimes work out how these weapons were used when the animals were alive.

The megalodon might have been the **largest meat eater** discovered so far.

Prehistoric weapons

Hard skeletons fossilize much better than the softer parts of an animal's body. This means that the remains of teeth and jaws are in a good-enough condition to give clear indications of the feeding habits of prehistoric animals.

Smilodon skull

Tyrannosaurus rex tooth

The *Tyrannosaurus* tooth was ridged to give it extra strength, and some could reach 11.8 in (30 cm) in length.

The Smilodon's canine teeth had cutting edges along both front and back and were 11 in (28 cm) long.

Megalodon tooth

Tyrannosaurus rex
This giant among meat-eating dinosaurs had the biggest teeth of any carnivore that has ever lived.

Smilodon
The massive canines of this saber-toothed cat may have been used to deliver deadly stabbing bites.

Megalodon
This shark may have grown four times bigger than today's great white shark—and have hunted whales.

PREHISTORIC BITES

The first backboned animals to evolve jaws were predatory fish—and they became the most formidable predators of their day. Since then, animals have evolved stronger jaws to cut through tough food, including flesh and bone. Scientists studying the skull structure of living and extinct animals can work out how jaws and their muscles produced impressive bite forces.

T-rex bite force
Although there were some bigger carnivorous dinosaurs, scientists estimate the *Tyrannosaurus rex* had the strongest bite of any land animal known.

Compared to animals alive today, the bite force of a *T-rex*—up to 60,000 N—is off the chart.

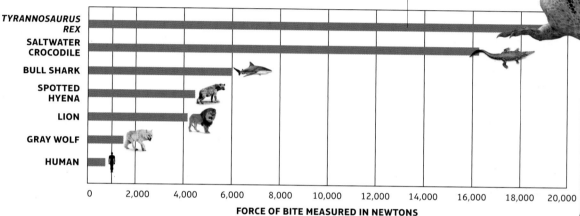

	FORCE OF BITE MEASURED IN NEWTONS
TYRANNOSAURUS REX	(off the chart)
SALTWATER CROCODILE	
BULL SHARK	
SPOTTED HYENA	
LION	
GRAY WOLF	
HUMAN	

0   2,000   4,000   6,000   8,000   10,000   12,000   14,000   16,000   18,000   20,000

FORCE OF BITE MEASURED IN NEWTONS

Great white shark tooth
Like many other meat-eaters, a great white's teeth have sawlike edges for slicing through flesh.

Great white shark
Today this species of shark is a top predator in oceans around the world.

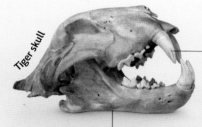

Tiger skull

The curved canines of a tiger are the longest of any living cat.

Tiger
Modern-day tigers, the largest of the big cats, are top predators on land.

RECORD BREAKERS

In the struggle to kill prey—or to stop being preyed upon—animals have evolved plenty of record-breaking qualities, from the deadliest of poisons to the fastest speeds, that set them apart in the natural world.

MUSCLES, JAWS, AND CLAWS

From the bite of a Siberian tiger to the squeeze of an anaconda, size and strength can be a deadly combination.

- **Largest living carnivore:** Sperm whale
- **Largest land carnivore:** Polar bear
- **Heaviest snake:** Green anaconda
- **Longest snake:** Reticulated python
- **Cat with biggest canine teeth:** Siberian tiger
- **Bird with longest claws:** Southern cassowary

Green anaconda

DEADLIEST STINGS AND POISONS

Some stings and poisons just inflict pain or discomfort, but a few—if left untreated—can be fatal.

Venomous stings that are deadliest to humans:
- **Jellyfish:** Sea wasp
- **Scorpion:** Deathstalker
- **Mollusk:** Cone snail
- **Fish:** Reef stonefish

Poison that is deadliest to humans:
- Golden poison frog

Deathstalker

RECORD-BREAKING TRAPS

Many animals create traps to catch prey. Whales blow bubbles to force shoals of fish to bunch into mouth-sized groups, while spiders spin webs to trap their prey.

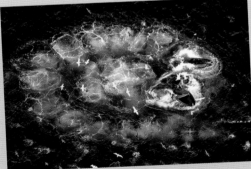

Humpback whale's bubble net

- **Biggest trap:** Bubble net of humpback whale
- **Biggest, strongest spider web:** Darwin's bark spider

DEADLIEST VENOMOUS BITES

The deadliest venoms harm the body by paralyzing muscles or causing internal bleeding, which can kill the victim.

Blue-ringed octopus

- **Most venomous snake:** Inland taipan
- **Most venomous spider:** Sydney funnel-web spider (male)
- **Most venomous mollusk:** Blue-ringed octopus

DECEIVERS AND TRICKSTERS

Sometimes trickery is needed to catch prey. Many animals use disguises or lures to entice prey to come closer.

- **Smartest spider:** Portia spider
- **Best disguised shark:** Tasselled wobbegong
- **Best disguised snake:** Puff adder
- **Smartest use of bait to catch fish:** Heron

Green heron

SKILLS, TACTICS, AND CUNNING

The fastest predators can catch the fastest prey, but many other special skills are used by a wide variety of hunters.

Cheetah

- **Sharpest insect vision:** Dragonfly
- **Deadliest electrical shock:** Electric eel
- **Fastest animal of all:** Peregrine falcon
- **Fastest sprinter:** Cheetah

DEADLY NUMBERS

Strength in numbers improves killing power—both for social insects, such as ants, and for bigger animals that hunt in packs.

Tropical American army ants

- **Deadliest stinging swarm:** Asian giant hornet
- **Most aggressive raiding ant:** Army ant
- **Largest social group of carnivorous land mammals:** Spotted hyena

DISEASE AND DESTRUCTION

Some animals kill by spreading disease, while others cause devastation by their aggression—destroying habitats and even wiping out other species.

Anopheles mosquito

- **Deadliest transmitter of human disease:** Female Anopheles mosquito
- **Most invasive amphibian:** Cane toad
- **Most invasive snake:** Brown tree snake
- **Most dangerously aggressive large mammal:** Hippopotamus

GLOSSARY

Abdomen
The belly of an animal or—in the case of an insect—the part of the body at its rear end that contains most of its vital organs.

Amphibians
A group of cold-blooded, backboned animals with moist skin. Frogs and toads are amphibians.

Antennae
Pairs of "feelers" attached to the head of an invertebrate animal, used for sensing its surroundings. The singular is antenna.

Arthropods
A group of invertebrates with jointed legs. Arthropods include insects, crustaceans, spiders, scorpions, centipedes, and millipedes.

Bait
Food which is used by an animal in a way to attract prey.

Bill
The hard part of a bird's mouth used for feeding, preening, and sometimes as a weapon in self-defense.

Camouflage
A way an animal blends into its surroundings so as not to be detected by predators or prey.

Carnivore
An animal that feeds on meat. Carnivores include wolves, hawks, and sharks.

Carrion
The flesh of dead animals.

Cooperative
Working together to achieve the same aim.

Crustaceans
A group of invertebrates with many jointed legs and often a shell. Crabs and shrimp are crustaceans.

Deep sea
Deep, dark parts of the ocean, usually deeper than 5,905 ft (1,800 m).

Disease
When the body doesn't work properly. Diseases are not caused directly by injury, but many—such as malaria—are spread by the bites of some kinds of animals.

Exoskeleton
The tough armorlike outer "skin" of some kinds of invertebrates. Insects, spiders, and crabs have an exoskeleton.

Extinct
When none of a particular species is alive today. Extinct kinds of animals lived in the past.

Filter-feeder
An animal that feeds by straining tiny particles of food from water. Many filter-feeders rely on plankton for food.

Fin
A flat extension to the body of an underwater animal used to help with control and steering while swimming.

Fossil
The preserved remains or impressions of dead organisms found in rock.

Gland
A small bag of fluid in the body. Venomous animals usually produce their venoms in glands.

Habitat
The place where an organism normally lives.

Herbivore
An animal that eats plants. Animals such as sheep, cattle, and deer are herbivores.

Ice floe
A large lump of floating ice, usually drifting on the ocean.

Insect
A six-legged animal with a body divided into three main regions: head, thorax, and abdomen. Most insects have wings and can fly, but some—such as worker ants—do not.

Introduced animal
An animal that has been put into a habitat that is not its

natural home. Humans have introduced rats, foxes, and other kinds of animals to different parts of the world.

Invasive animal
An animal that rapidly increases in numbers in a particular place, often causing harm.

Invertebrate
An animal without a backbone, such as a snail or an insect.

Larva
A young stage of an animal that looks very different from its adult form. A caterpillar is the larva stage of a butterfly. The plural is larvae.

Mammal
A group of warm-blooded, air-breathing backboned animals, usually covered with hair. Cats, hippopotamuses, and humans are mammals.

Mimic
To copy. Animals pretend to be animals or other objects to hide from danger, to attract prey, or to scare away predators.

Mollusks
A group of invertebrates with a soft body, sometimes held in a protective shell. Snails, clams, octopuses, and squid are mollusks.

Organism
Any living thing, including plants and animals.

Paralyze
When there is harm caused to muscles so they can no longer work to make the body move.

Parasite
An organism that gets food, or some other benefit, by living on another organism called its host, and causes the host harm.

Plankton
Tiny living organisms that float in open water, as they cannot swim against the currents.

Poison
A substance that harms an organism if swallowed or touched.

Predator
An animal that kills another animal (its prey) to feed on it.

Prey
An animal that is killed by a predator.

Pride
A group of lions.

Range
The geographical area where an animal lives in the wild.

Raptor
A bird of prey, such as an eagle, a falcon, or an owl.

Reef
A colony of ocean animals called corals that form rocky growths under the water.

Reptiles
A group of cold-blooded, air-breathing, backboned animals with scaly skin. Crocodiles, snakes, and lizards are reptiles.

Shellfish
Any underwater invertebrate animal with a shell, such as a crab or a clam.

Shoal
A group of fish, or other underwater animals of the same kind, that swim together.

Siphon
A tube for sucking in or pumping out water.

Stinger
Sharp, stabbing weapon of an animal used for injecting venom.

Tentacle
The very long grasping "arm" of an invertebrate, such as a jellyfish, octopus, or squid.

Toxic
The effects of a harmful chemical substance, such as a poison or a venom.

Venom
A substance that harms the body when it is injected through a bite or a sting.

Vertebrate
An animal with a backbone, such as a fish or a mammal.

INDEX

ACKNOWLEDGMENTS

Dorling Kindersley would like to thank the following: Charvi Arora, Bharti Bedi, and Neha Samuel for editorial assistance; Spencer Holbrook, Roshni Kapur, and Anjali Sachar for design assistance; Vishal Bhatia, Jaypal Singh Chauhan, Satish Gaur, Nityanand Kumar, and Anurag Trivedi for technical assistance; Deepak Negi, Nishwan Rasool, and Surya Sankash Sarangi for picture research assistance; Hazel Beynon for proofreading; and Margaret McCormack for the index.

Picture Credits

The publisher would like to thank the following for their kind permission to reproduce their photographs:

(Key: a-above; b-below/bottom; c-center; f-far; l-left; r-right; t-top)

2 Getty Images: Roger de la Harpe (l). **3 Alamy Stock Photo:** Nature Picture Library (c). **4 Dreamstime.com:** Sergey Uryadnikov (tl). **Getty Images:** Ian Waldie / Staf (tr). **naturepl.com:** Visuals Unlimited (br). **5 iStockphoto.com:** Ginosphotos (tl). **Robert Harding Picture Library:** Christian Valle (tr). **6 Alamy Stock Photo:** Ernie Janes (bl). **FLPA:** Thomas Marent (tl); Mark Moffett (tr). **naturepl.com:** Will Burrard-Lucas (br). **7 FLPA:** Anup Shah / Minden Pictures (tl). **Getty Images:** Ingo Arndt / Minden Pictures (bl); Gunter Ziesler (tr). **8 Alamy Stock Photo:** imageBROKER. **Dreamstime.com:** Photomyeye (c). **Getty Images:** Mark Moffett / Minden Pictures (cla). **9 Alamy Stock Photo:** Blickwinkel (clb); Geoff du Feu (bc). **Getty Images:** Ch'ien Lee / Minden Pictures (crb); Frank Pali (cla); Mametrahardi (c); Stephen Osman (cr); Stumayhew (bl). **naturepl.com:** Jurgen Freund (ca); Rod Williams (cb). **10-11 Dreamstime.com:** Sergey Uryadnikov. **13 naturepl.com:** David Fleetham. **14-15 FLPA:** ImageBroker. **14 Getty Images:** Tim Laman (bl). **16 Getty Images:** Piotr Naskrecki / Minden Pictures. **17 Dreamstime.com:** Leopoldo Palomba (clb); Photomyeye. **18 Getty Images:** Jim Abernethy (cra); Alexander Safonov. **19 iStockphoto.com:** Kurga. **20 Alamy Stock Photo:** Nature Picture Library. **21 Getty Images:** Mike Parry / Minden Pictures. **22 © Alejandro Arteaga. Tropical Herping.. 23 FLPA:** Yva Momatiuk & John Eastcott / Minden Pictures (tr). **iStockphoto.com:** CraigRJD. **24-25 Getty Images:** Michael Dunning.

24 Alamy Stock Photo: Mike Lane (clb). **26 Dreamstime.com:** Nikolay Grachev. **naturepl.com:** Jurgen Freund (cra). **27 Depositphotos Inc:** stephstarr9363@gmail.com. **28 Getty Images:** Andy Rouse. **29 Getty Images:** David Tipling. **30 Getty Images:** Danita Delimont. **31 Getty Images:** Frank Pali. **32 Getty Images:** Tom Brakefield (crb). **Francisco Herrera / www.flickr.com/ photos/39273888@N00/. 33 Getty Images:** Manfred Delpho (crb). **Paul Sangeorzan. 34 Bruce Fryxell:** https://www.flickr.com/photos/bfryxell/ albums/. **Getty Images:** Sylvain Cordier. **35 Getty Images:** Franco Banfi. **36-37 Getty Images:** Ian Waldie / Staf. **38 Alamy Stock Photo:** imageBROKER. **39 Science Photo Library:** Steve Gschmeissner. **40-41 Getty Images:** Joel Sartore, National Geographic Photo Ark. **42 Alamy Stock Photo:** Ken Griffiths. **43 Science Photo Library:** Robert Noonan. **44 Getty Images:** Ian Waldie / Staff. **45 Getty Images:** Mametrahardi. **46 Getty Images:** Matthijs Kuijpers; Oliver Lucanus / NiS / Minden Pictures. **47 Alamy Stock Photo:** Matthijs Kuijpers (cl). **naturepl.com:** Visuals Unlimited. **48 Bhavya Joshi - www.bhavyajoshi.com / https://500px.com/bhavya: . 49 Dan Rosenberg:** (cra). **Günter Leitenbauer** www.leitenbauer.net. **50 Getty Images:** Roger de la Harpe. **51 Alamy Stock Photo:** Ken Griffiths. **52-53 iStockphoto.com:** 13672071.

53 iStockphoto.com: Denis_Prof (tc). **54 FLPA:** Chris & Tilde Stuart. **55 Getty Images:** Thomas Marent / Minden Pictures. **56-57 iStockphoto.com:** Ginosphotos. **58 Getty Images:** Auscape. **59 Getty Images:** Marka. **60-61 Getty Images:** Norbert Wu / Minden Pictures (b). **naturepl.com:** Visuals Unlimited (t). **62 SuperStock:** Fred Bavendam / Minden Pictures. **63 Todd Aki / https://www.flickr.com/photos/90966819@N00/albums:** (cra). **Getty Images:** Brandi Mueller. **64 iStockphoto.com:** Captainsecret. **65 Getty Images:** Stephen Osman. **66 Ozgur Kerem Bulur / https://www.flickr.com/ photos/70091193@N06/. 67 Michael A. Cruz. 68 Ardea:** Scott Camazine / Science Source. **69 Getty Images:** George Grall. **70-71 stevebloom.com:** Franðois Gilson. **71 Alamy Stock Photo:** Hemis (cr). **72 Getty Images:** Mark Moffett / Minden Pictures. **73 naturepl.com:** Martin Dohrn. **74 Science Photo Library:** Francesco Tomasinelli. **75 Getty Images:** Jonathan Bird. **76 123RF.com:** Aquafun. **77 Getty Images:** Franco Banfi (tr); Chris Newbert / Minden Pictures. **78-79 Getty Images:** Eco / UIG. **80 Alamy Stock Photo:** Hemis. **81 FLPA:** Gerry Ellis. **82 naturepl.com:** Sylvain Cordier. **83 Getty Images:** Thomas Marent / Minden Pictures. **84 FLPA:** Daniel Heuclin. **85 Getty Images:** Minden Pictures (clb). **naturepl.com:** Dave Watts. **86-87 Robert Harding Picture Library:** Christian Valle. **88 Getty Images:** Norbert Wu / Minden Pictures. **89 Ilan lubitz underwater photographer. Diving since 1956. Lives in the Philippines. 90 Alamy Stock Photo:** Blickwinkel. **91 Alamy Stock Photo:** Andrew Mackay. **92-93 Alamy Stock Photo:** Genevieve Vallee. **93 Science Photo Library:** B.G. Thomson (tr). **94-95 Ardea:** James H. Robinson / Science Sour (t). **SuperStock:** Michael & Patricia Fogden / Minden Pictures (b). **95 Alamy Stock Photo:** Marcel Strelow (bc). **96 Getty Images:** Piotr Naskrecki / Minden Pictures (br). **naturepl.com:** Brent Stephenson. **97 Alamy Stock Photo:** Design Pics Inc. **SeaPics.com:** Masakazu Ushioda (cr). **98-99 FLPA:** Thomas Marent. **100 Alamy Stock Photo:** Arco Images GmbH; Arto Hakola (t). **101 Getty Images:** Mark Moffett / Minden Pictures. **102 Alamy Stock Photo:** B. Mete Uz. **103 FLPA:** Thomas Marent / Minden Pictures. **104 Dorling Kindersley:** Frank Greenaway / Natural History Museum, London (cr). **Getty Images:** Darlyne A. Murawski. **105 Getty Images:** Ullstein bild. **106-107 Science Photo Library:** Dante Fenolio. **108 Alamy Stock Photo:** Blickwinkel. **109 Getty Images:** Oliver Lucanus / NiS / Minden Pictures. **110 Getty Images:** Ullstein Bild. **naturepl.com:** Georgette Douwma (cra). **111 Getty Images:** Mark Webster (cra). **iStockphoto.com:** Cinoby. **112 Alamy Stock Photo:** Ryan M. Bolton. **113 Ardea:** Kenneth W Fink. **114 naturepl.com:** Rod Williams. **115 SuperStock:** NaturePL. **116 Alamy Stock Photo:** Eng Wah Teo. **117 123RF.com:** Dave Montreuil (bl). **Alamy Stock Photo:** Ernie Janes. **118 FLPA:** Alan Murphy, BIA (clb); Donald M. Jones / Minden Pictures. **119 naturepl.com:** T.J. RICH. **120-121 naturepl.com:** Andy Rouse. **122 naturepl.com:** Shattil & Rozinski. **123 Getty Images:** Theo Allofs (clb); Martin Ruegner. **124-125 FLPA:** Mark Moffett. **126-127 Getty Images:** Adek Berry / Stringer (b). **OceanwideImages.com:** C & M Fallows (t). **127 Getty Images:** Reinhard Dirscherl (br). **128 Getty Images:** Borut Furlan. **129 iStockphoto.com:** Mark_Doh. **130 Virginia Settepani / http://www.spiderlab.dk. 131 iStockphoto.com:** TacioPhilip. **132 Getty Images:** Alastair Macewen. **133 Getty Images:** Ch'ien Lee / Minden Pictures. **134 naturepl.com:** Konrad Wothe. **135 Getty Images:** Mallardg500. **136-137 Getty Images:** Tambako the Jaguar. **138 Alamy Stock Photo:** Octavio Campos Salles (cr). **Getty Images:** Tambako the Jaguar. **139 naturepl.com:** Will Burrard-Lucas. **140 Dreamstime.com:** Glenn Nagel (br). **Getty Images:** PHOTO 24. **141 Dreamstime.com:** John Platt (br). **naturepl.com:** Tony Heald. **142-143 Getty Images:** Gallo Images. **144-145 FLPA:** Anup Shah / Minden Pictures.

146-147 Paul Bertner - www.rainforests.smugmug.com: (b). **SeaPics.com:** Andy Murch (t). **148-149 Getty Images:** Tim Perceval. **150 Alamy Stock Photo:** Prisma by Dukas Presseagentur GmbH. **Avalon:** Paulo de Oliveira (cra). **151 Getty Images:** Danita Delimont. **152 Markus Oulehla. 153 FLPA:** Jelger Herder, Buiten-beeld. **154 naturepl.com:** Sylvain Cordier. **155 naturepl.com:** Guy Edwardes. **156-157 Alamy Stock Photo:** Nature Picture Library. **158 Mike Jackson. 159 Rudi Petitjean. 160 Getty Images:** Auscape. **161 Getty Images:** Henny Brandsma / Buiten-beeld / Minden Pictures. **162 Getty Images:** Stumayhew. **163 Getty Images:** Jeff Rotman. **164-165 Getty Images:** Suzi Eszterhas / Minden Pictures. **166-167 Getty Images:** Gunter Ziesler. **168 Alamy Stock Photo:** Photo Resource Hawaii. **169 Alamy Stock Photo:** Frank Hecker. **170 Alamy Stock Photo:** Roger Eritja (cl); Geoff du Feu (r). **171 Jan Anderson https://www.flickr.com/photos/40132175@N06/:** (cr). **Science Photo Library:** B. G. Thomson. **172 Science Photo Library:** Martin Dohrn. **173 Science Photo Library:** John Burbidge. **174 Science Photo Library:** Alex Wild / Visuals Unlimited, Inc.. **175 Getty Images:** Sirachai Arunrugstichai. **176 Getty Images:** Nick Garbutt / Nature Picture Library; Joel Sartore, National Geographic Ark (cra). **177 Science Photo Library:** Mark Smith. **178 SeaPics.com:** David B. Fleetham. **179 iStockphoto.com:** Reptiles4all. **180 Getty Images:** Ch'ien Lee / Minden Pictures. **181 Getty Images:** Derek Middleton / FLPA / Minden Pictures. **182-183 Getty Images:** Samuel Betkowski. **183 Getty Images:** Johner Images (t). **184 Getty Images:** Ambre Haller. **185 Getty Images:** Sergey Gorshkov / Minden Pictures. **186-187 Getty Images:** Nick Garbutt. **188 Alaskaphotographics.com:** Patrick J Endres. **189 FLPA:** Sean Crane. **190-191 Getty Images:** Barcroft Media. **192-193 Getty Images:** Theo Allofs / Minden Pictures. **194 Getty Images:** Ingo Arndt / Minden Pictures (bl); Thomas Marent / Minden Pictures (cr). **195 Getty Images:** John Cancalosi; Joe McDonald (ca); Bianca Lavies (cra). **196 Alamy Stock Photo:** Grant Heilman Photography (bc). **Getty Images:** Carol Farneti-Foster (br); Joel Sartore (cra); Buddy Mays (cra). **197 Alamy Stock Photo:** Nature Picture Library (cla); Survivalphotos (br). **Getty Images:** Don Johnston (bc); Robert Oelman (cra); Susan Walker (bl). **naturepl.com:** Martin Dohrn (ca). **198 123RF.com:** Matthew Ragen (c). **Dreamstime.com:** Geoffrey Kuchera (cl); Jason Ondreicka (bl). **Getty Images:** Michael & Patricia Fogden / Minden Pictures (clb). **199 Dorling Kindersley:** Linda Pitkin (crb/ surgeonfish). **Dreamstime.com:** Martin Maritz (clb); Seanjeeves (crb). **Getty Images:** Art Wolfe (cr); Nick Garbutt (cla); Thomas Marent / Visuals Unlimted, Inc. (cra); Paul Nicklen (c); Paul Souders (bl). **iStockphoto.com:** CarGe (tr); Takeo1775 (ca). **200 Dorling Kindersley:** Colin Keates / Natural History Museum, London (c); Harry Taylor / Natural History Museum, London (cl, crb). **Dreamstime.com:** Sofia Santos / Chastity (bl). **201 Dorling Kindersley:** Harry Taylor / Natural History Museum, London (clb); Jerry Young (cla). **Dreamstime.com:** Andrea Crisante (tr); Iakov Filimonov (cra); Leopoldo Palomba (bl). **Getty Images:** Jim Abernethy (ca). **202 Alamy Stock Photo:** imageBROKER (bc). **© Alejandro Arteaga. Tropical Herping:** (cl). **Getty Images:** Stephen Osman (tr). **Robert Harding Picture Library:** Christian Valle (br). **203 Alamy Stock Photo:** Roger Eritja (br). **FLPA:** Donald M. Jones / Minden Pictures (tl). **Getty Images:** Andy Rouse (tr). **naturepl.com:** Konrad Wothe (bl)

All other images © Dorling Kindersley
For further information see: www.dkimages.com